FOREWORD.

The purpose in writing this grammar has been to give
the student a handbook of Middle English in which the
chief features of the language and literature of the
period would be presented as clearly and concisely as possible.

I have felt that a grammar such as Wright's"Elementary
Middle English Grammar" lays too much stress on the
background of the M.E. period,while it does not under-
line sufficiently the O.E. beginnings of the dialectal
divergences which became so important in M.E. Moreover,the treatment of the M.E. dialects themselves becomes obscured in too much detail,as far as the beginner
is concerned. This is true,not only of Wright,but also
of Wyld,Luick,Jordan and even Moore.

In an attempt to overcome this defect,I have treated the
dialects on a very broad plane,constantly stressing those
salient features of the different dialects which will
enable the student to identify them easily.

Another characteristic of Moore and Wyld to which I take
exception,is their insistance upon the E.Midland dialect
to the neglect of the others. I feel this to be a mis-
take for two reasons.First,there is a sufficiently large

body of writings in the M.E. period in dialects other than
E.Mid. that the student should have some knowledge of their
accidence and its dialectal peculiarities. Secondly,if the
whole dialectal picture is lost,it becomes much more difficult for the student to grasp the development of the
literary standard language,and many thihgs in it are un-
oplained,for all of the dialects contributed something to
modern speech.

In the treatment of accidence,then,there is ,in Moore,
a lack of dialectal differentiation;in Wyld,too much une
sorted information.A further hiatus in both is syntax.Too
little attention is paid to the form in which the words
of the literary dialect arranged themselves.I have attemp-
ted to give some outline of this subject.

Finally,Middle English Grammars in general are too prone
to divorce themselves from the literature of the period.I
have tried to bring the language and the literature togct-
her,once more under dialectal headings,so that the student
may correlate his knowledge of the grammar with the works
from which we gain our information of the grammar.

AN OUTLINE OF MIDDLE ENGLISH GRAMMAR.

TABLE OF CONTENTS.

AN OUTLINE OF MIDDLE ENGLISH GRAMMER

CHAPTER 1. The Middle English Period

(I) The M.E. period extends from about 1100 (the transition
period) to about 1450 (the beginning of modern English),[1] and
the various aspects of the language of this period may be studied
in a general way under the headings of the five great dialects:
Northern, West Midland, East Midland, South Western and Kentish.
The first three correspond to O.E. Angl., the second to W.S. and
the third, Kentish.

At the beginning of the M.E. period, S.W. was the outstanding dialect, since its equivalent - W.S. - had become the
literary language of O.E. However, during the M.E. period, S.W.
gradually gives place to E.Mid. in importance. By the beginning
of the 14th century, Mid. forms have ousted many S.W. forms in
the south, and by the end of the 14th century London speech, at
any rate, is preponderantly E.Mid., and that dialect has become
the literary one. It is really, then, from E.Mid. that modern
English springs.[2]

(I.1) Differences between O.E. and M.E. Although we are
considering only five dialects in the M.E. period, there were
in fact many more. The increase in the number of dialects is
one of the most noticeable differences between O.E. and M.E. It
was largely due to the normal developments of dialectal
differences in O.E., although the new changes in the actual M.E.

period did add considerably to the num'er of di(f)lects. In fact,
there were almost as many dialects as there were to.ns and,
naturally, with a certain amount of intercourse between various
districts, there arose some confusion in dialectal forms. ..ence,
it is not surprising to find Mid. forms in S.'. texts, or Nth.
forms in 'id. texts.   It is to be understood, therefore, that
any dialectal b undaries must be arbitrary, althoigh for
practical purposes we shall consider them as fixed. The student
must also realise that in a text called, for instance, ~. . all
the forms will not be of that dialect, but will be mixed with
many forms from Mid. and even some from Nth., but t e greater
number of forms will be characteristically S.'. Again, it is
i p ssible to say that any one change took place at a certain
date, for the change in langua e is necessarily gradual, but
for practical purposes we shall fix upon certain dates in or ou
to give so e idea of chronological development during the period.
In this connection, it will be impossible to consider the
various t'eories of recent scholars concerning the probable
periods of sound change,[*5] and so, for the ti e being at least,
t'e older, acce ted t'eories will be followed. 'is limita ion
is particularly relative to the develop e t of now di ht'ro n in
.'. Therefore in orde to consider t'e whole tter br a ly, we
shall confine our attention to the five great dialects of '
period, . ' we shall accept arbitrary limitations as to bou i s
a   eriods of develo ment.

One of the greatest changes from O.E. to M.E. is the change in orthography. The change is largely owing to Anglo-Norman scribes who substituted their own symbols for native ones, and made new symbols for unfamiliar sounds. [*4] The most striking of such changes are: the loss of the O.E. symbols æ, ƿ and ð (with the adoption of the th symbol in place of the last two); the use of u for O.E. cw; and the new modes of spelling the O.E. front 3 -

There were also many changes in pronunciation during the M.E. period, and chief among them were the development of new 'diphth'ongs and the weakening of unstressed syllables. Not only the vowels of inflectional endings, but also those of other unstressed syllables were affected by this weakening. The loss of inflectional endings was greatest in the [*5] north and east, where the Scandinavians settled. Here, the root words were essential, but the endings were disregarded. The result was that the differences between the various noun declensions disappeared so that, by the end of the period, all nouns had gone over to the old 'a' declension. The verbs, also, had lost many of their endings.

The loss of case endings led to the development of a new system of syntax in which prepositions were substituted for endings, and precision of word order became compulsory.

To these changes in the language must be added the great changes in vocabulary owing to extensive borrowings from the French and Scandinavian tongues. Since French was the language of the court, by far the greater number of borrowings

in the south came from the French, but in the north and east,
where the Danes had settled extensively, there is a large body
of Scandinavian borrowings.   Vocabulary is thus an important
dialectal difference between north and south.

(I.2) Analogy. [6]   Analogy is the building up of new
forms on the pattern of forms already existing.   The result of
this action may be seen chiefly in three ways:

(a) in inflected cases in which the vowel of one form is
carried through into another form.   For instance, in "M." a new
plural-daies- was formed on the analogy of the singular in the
noun 'dai', whereas the logical plural form should have been
'dawes' (from the O. . plural 'dagas') and this form does occur
in some dialects.   In such a case the action of analogy is
also termed levelling.

(b) in the inflectional endings themselves.   There was a
general reformation of the inflectional system, owing to which
the majority of "M." nouns were inflected on the analogy of the
O. . 'a' stems;- the 'a' ending of the genitive singular of O. .
'sunu' became, through analogy with the 'a' stems, 'es' in "M.".
The same type of change is to be found frequently in . . verbs.

(c) in the creation of derivatives such as adverbs from
already existing nouns or adjectives.   An example of this may be
seen in the '. . adverb 'pertely' which is formed from the O.
French 'apert' and the O. . 'lic'.

(2) Dialectal characteristics. There are certain
features in the various dialects which are virtually sign-posts
for them. Among these are: Nth., the retention of ā; the
writing au or ghu for O.E. ēaw; and the present participle in -
ande instead of -ende; and the -'es' of the present indicative
of verbs; in Mid., the present participle in -ende, and the
present indicative plural in -en; in Sth., the present
participle in -inde; and the present indicative plural in -e
or -eth; in W.Mid. and S.W. the change of y to ü; in E. Mid.
and S.W., the development of the O.E. eo üi_htlong to ö ;
and in Kt., the rising diphthong and the change of y to e.

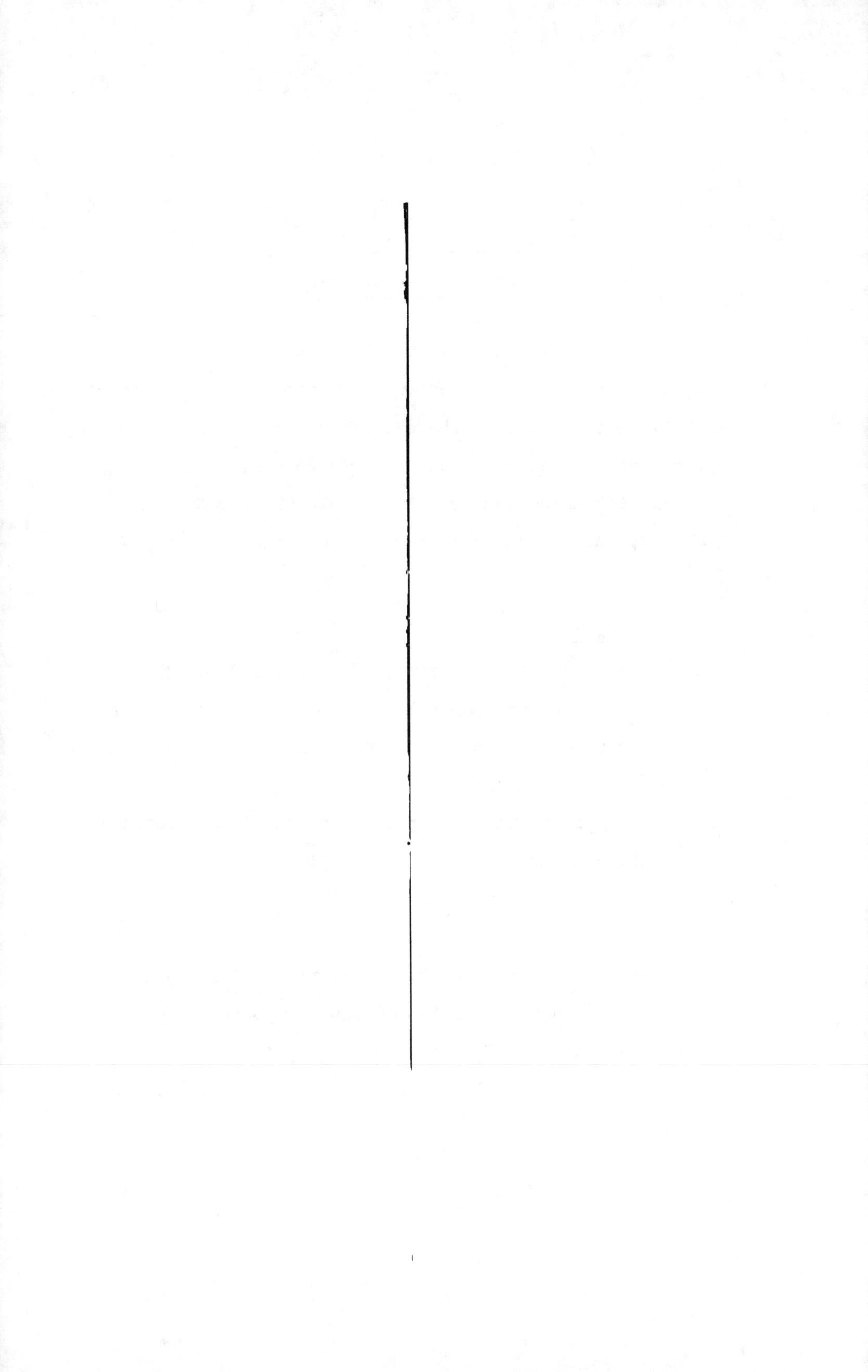

C h a p t e r II

The Chief Dialectal Differences In O.E.

(3) In order to understand fully the dialectal differences in W.S., it is necessary to review the differences which developed, not in W.S., but in O.E.   These differences can be grouped under the various sound changes which occurred in O.E., chiefly: Breaking, Diphthongisation by Initial Palatal, i/j Umlaut, u/o/a Umlaut, and the changes brought about through the influence of w. [*7]

(3.1) Breaking [*8]

This change affected the vowels ǽ, ě, ǐ and was the result of the action of the consonants l, r, h plus consonant and h single. It occurred much more regularly in W.S. and Kt. than in Angl. (Mercian and Northern).

The breaking of ae before l plus consonant is the least regular, occurring uniformly only in W.S.   In Angl. and Kt., the ae regularly retracted to a, though in L.Kt. there are instances of breaking to ea.

Otherwise, breaking occurred regularly, but in Angl., the resulting diphthongs smoothed to monophthongs before the consonant groups lh, lc, lȝ, rh, rc, rȝ.

The dialectal forms due to breaking would therefore be as follows:

		W.S.	Kt.	Angl.
æ	plus l	ea	a(L.Kt.ea)	a
	plus r	ea	ea	ea(sm. rh,re,rʒ)--ao/e
	plus h	ea	ea	ea(sm. al...a) ---ao/e
e	plus le/lh only	eo	eo	eo(sm. le, lh)---- e
		oo	eo	eo(sm. rh,re,rʒ)---e
		eo	eo	eo(sm. always) ----e
i	plus l	no breaking in any dialect		
	plus r	io	io	io(sm. rh,re,rʒ) --i
	plus h	io	io	io(sm. always) ---- i
ǣ	plus h	ēa	ēa	ēa(sm. always)----- ē
ī	plus h	īo	īo	īo(sm. alw..a)----- ī

(3.2) <u>Diphthongisation by Initial Palatal.</u> [*8]

This change is limited to W.S. It concerns the vowels
ǣ and ē̆, and is affected by the initial consonants c, ʒ, sc and j.

	W.S.	Kt.	Angl.
æ	ea	ea/e	æ
ǣ	ēa	ē	ē
e	ie	e	e
ē	īe	ē	ē

(3.3) <u>i/j Umlaut.</u> [*8]

All dialects were affected by i/j umlaut, but there were
certain differences in the results. In Kt. æ umlauted to e instead
of remaining at the æ stage as in the other dialects; and ū became
ȳ̆ in Kt. instead of ȳ. Kt. and Angl. have an umlauting of ēa to
ē (occasionally in Angl. ea--æ), and in those dialects the ... o
umlauting of īo, though forms with ēo are found. I.. all
diphthongs, ēa,ēo,īo are umlauted to the characteristic ... īo.

W.S.	Kt.	Angl.
a	ǣ	ǣo
ea	ȳe	ǣ (occas. ōa--ǣe).
īo	īe	īo/ōo

(5.4) <u>u/o/a Umlaut.</u>

By this change, the vowels a,e,i, were diphthongised by a
following a,o,u.   This action was greatly limited in W.S., and
only occurred there with any regularity through intervening
labial consonants p,b,f,m, and the liquids l,r.   The results
of the change are to be seen most widely in Angl., where it
acted through all consonants.

(5.5) <u>The Influence of w.</u> [8]

In L.W.S., weo/wio became wu, or occasionally wo.
In Kth., we became woo or wo.

(5.6) <u>Monophthongisation.</u> [8]

The two important developments to notice here are those in
.. n in Angl.   In W.S. the īo diphthong (which was
practically confined to this dialect) became ȳ or ī. In Angl.
all diphthongs were smoothed before h, ʒ , or c, whether these
consonants were immediately following or in the groups
lc,lʒ , rc, r ʒ , rh.

(4) <u>Examples of Dialectal Differences in O.E.</u>

<u>Breaking.</u>

	W.S.	Kt.	Angl.
*æo ll	eall	all	all
*wero	weore	weore	weore--wero
*nāoh	nēah	nēah	nēah--nēh

<u>Diphthongisation</u>

	W.S.	Kt.	Angl.
ʒæt	ʒeat	ʒet	ʒæt/ ʒet
ʒēt	ʒīet	ʒēt	ʒēt

<u>i/j Umlaut.</u>

	W.S.	Kt.	Angl.
× clūni	clǣne	clēne	clǣne
*fullan	fyllan	r.Kt.fyllan	fyllan
		L.Kt.fellan	
*carrjan	cierran	cerran	cerran
*hirdjaz	hierde	hiorde	hiorde
			(Merc. hoorde)

<u>u/o/a Umlaut.</u>

	W.S.	Kt.	Angl.
gatu	geatu	gatu	geatu
nodu	nedu	neodu	nodu
*hofon	heofon	heofon	heofon

<u>Influence of w.</u>

	W.S.	Kt.	Angl.
widu	wiodu-wudu	wiodu	wiodu
wosan	wosan	wesan	wesan (Nth. wosn)

<u>Mono hthongisation.</u>

	W.S.	Kt.	Angl.
× reht	reoht-rioht	reoht	reoht/reht
	-riht/ryht		

CHAPTER III

M. E. Changes: Introduction

(5)   Syllables.

A syllable must have one vowel sound, and may have
one or more consonant sounds.

(5.1) The division of syllables. In words of more than one
syllable, the division comes: (1) after the vowel and before
the consonant when only one consonant separates the vowels -
e.g. Sa/xon, fe/la/ e; (2) between the consonants when two of
them separate the vowels - e.g. en/Lang, let/tyng; (3) after
the first consonant when three consonants separate the vowels -
e.g. fyl/the, shul/dre.

(5.2) Long and short syllables. A long syllable is one which
contains a long vowel or diphthong - e.g. stōn, nā/me - or one
which is terminated by two consonants - e.g. fast, hand. All
other syllables are short - e.g. that, sor/we.

(5.3) Open and close syllables. An open syllable is one which
is terminated by a vowel - e.g. thū/hen, hō/li. (All words in
which only one consonant separates two vowels will have at least
one open syllable.) A close syllable is one which is terminated
by a consonant - e.g. grim/li, at.

(5.4) sc and st. It is important to note that the consonant
groups sc and st are not considered as double consonants
except where they occurred initially or finally as in best or

consonants, and hence syllabic division came before the group,
and the preceding vowel was in an open syllable - e.g. ca/stely.

(6) <u>Vowels and Consonants.</u>

The manner in which vowels and consonants were pronounced and the position of the organs of the throat and mouth
at the moment of their pronunciation, determine the nature of
the sounds and therefore determine their development.

(6.I) <u>Open and close vowels.</u> (N.B. These must not be confused
with open and close syllables). The difference between open
and close vowels is determined by the nearness of the tongue to
the roof of the mouth when pronouncing them.   hen an open $\bar{ę}$ (ɛ)
is pronounced, the space between the tongue and the roof of the
mouth is greater than when a close $\bar{ẹ}$ (e:) is formed. The signs
generally used to indicate these qualities in a vowel are: a
hook under a vowel to show that it is open - ę, and a period to
show that it is closed - ẹ.

(6.2) <u>Front and back vowels.</u> The front vowels are ae, e, i, -
in the pronunciation of which the tongue approaches the front of
the roof. The back vowels are a,o,u, in the pronunciation of
which the tongue approaches the back of the roof. The tongue is
also raised higher for some vowels than for others, and the
accompanying diagram shows the relative positions of both
front and back vowels

         Front   i   y   u   Back

                     e   ɔ   o

                        ae - a

The semi-vowel, y, stands, in pronunciation, half-way between the highest front and the highest back vowels.

(6.3) <u>Round and Unround vowels.</u> These terms indicate the position of the lips when a vowel is pronounced. Vowels such as o (o:) and a (u:) are called <u>round</u> vowels because the lips are rounded in pronouncing them; but the vowels ē (e:), ī (i:) are <u>unround</u> vowels because there is no rounding of the lips when they are pronounced. The round and unround qualities of vowels differ with different dialects, for in some dialects such as N.Mid. and S.W., there is a greater tendency to round the lips than in other dialects. Hence, a vowel may undergo rounding or unrounding according to the dialects.

(6.4) <u>Voiced and voiceless sounds.</u> Voiced sounds are produced by compressing the vocal chords, but when the chords are in a normal, relaxed state, the sounds produced are <u>voiceless</u>. All vowel sounds are voiced, but the consonants vary. The difference between the voiced and voiceless sounds may be illustrated by the difference in pronunciation between s and z, f and v. In these groups, s and f are the voiceless sounds and z and v are the voiced ones.

(6.5) <u>Explosive and continuant consonants.</u> Explosive (or stop) consonants are formed by forcing the breath through the mouth passage which is momentarily closed - e.g. b,p,d. Continuant (or open) consonants are those in which the breath has no hindrance, although the passage is somewhat narrowed - e.g. f,s,t.

(6.6)   <u>Front and back consonants</u>. (N.B. These consonants are frequently called palatal and guttural).[10.] Front consonants are pronounced with the front of the tongue, while back consonants are formed between the back of the tongue and the soft palate. The nature of these consonants was often determined in O. E. and M. E. by the accompanying vowel sounds, and therefore, in M. E., the consonants c,g,h, are to be found as both front and back sounds.   Each form of the consonant has a different history - e.g.c.   Back c became k in M. E., while front c became ch.

7.   <u>Table of sounds.</u>   Wherever possible, the usual written symbol of the sound is retained as the phonetic symbol, but where it has been necessary to differentiate between closely allied sounds, special symbols have been introduced on the authority of other grammarians. The vowels which need closest attention are the $\bar{e}$'s, $\bar{o}$'s, and u's. Only those consonants whose sound is not indicated by the written letter have been listed. The colon - : - indicates length.

	xample	ymbol	Modern Approximation	Example	Symbol	Modern Approximation
æ	hae tt(O.E.)	ae	hat	huerte (3)	∅	r. peu
ǣ	'ae r (O....)	ae: *ll		duep (3)	∅:	' houreuse
a	appel (.E.)	a Germ.	<u>a</u>pel	kun (E.)	y	" juste
ā	dale "	a:	father	prude (E.)	y:	'
ē	mete "	ε:	<u>ai</u>ry	_Consonants_		
ō	mode '	o:	th<u>ey</u>	c calf ("....)	k	<u>c</u>alf
e	bed "	e	bed	o cese "	tʃ	<u>ch</u>eese
i	ring "	i	ring	cg/ff brugge '	dʒ	<u>bri</u>gge
ī	five "	i:	mach<u>i</u>ne	ʒ ʒ ard '	j	<u>y</u>ara
o	flok '	ə	flock	h sah '	x	Scot. lo<u>ch</u>
ɔ	ston "	ɒ:	sh<u>a</u>wl	ng thing "	ŋ	thi<u>ng</u>
ɔ	fot "	o:	n<u>o</u>te	s risen "	z	ri<u>s</u>en
u	ful '	u	full	sh ship "	ʃ	<u>sh</u>ip
ū	hus "	u:	r<u>u</u>de	ba f	θ	ba<u>th</u>
	obscure vowel	ə	weath<u>er</u>	brođer	đ	bro<u>th</u>er

CHAPTER   IV

Orthographic   Changes.

(8)   The majority of orthographic changes in M.E. were the result of the influence of the scribes, both Anglo-Norman and those native scribes who belonged to the educated classes and were familiar with the Anglo-Norman modes of spelling.[+13.]

(8.I)   The large number of changes in M.E. is further to be explained by the fact that, during the O.E. period, there had been many sound changes so that, by the end of the period, the old symbols no longer indicated truly the sounds for which they stood. For instance, O.E. diphthongs had smoothed by the end of the period and yet diphthongic symbols were still used; in the consonants, front c had become t∫ in sound by the IIth century, but O.E. c was still used for it.

(8.2)   Apart from those symbols which expressed the sounds inadequately, there were other symbols which were unfamiliar to the Anglo-Norman scribes, and these disappeared altogether. Such were æ, þ, and ð, and the runic . They were replaced by different symbols representing the same sounds. Moreover, even when the symbols were not unfamiliar, but when the same sound was written differently in French, the French scribes preferred their own symbols. Thus, O.E. cw was replaced by qu. Other changes were made in the attempt to differentiate between two or more sounds which, in O.E. were expressed by

the same symbol. . . . front c̜ was, in sound tʃ ; while
O.E. back c̜ was, in sound ɑ. Again, there was a tendency to
differentiate between sounds similarly formed, in order to
prevent confusion. Hence, in combinations of u̲ ith m/n, or
of i̲ ith m/n, u̲ as often written o̲ and i̲ was often written y̲.
(8.3) There is great orthographic confusion in M.E. since
there was no definite literary standard to fix the mode of
spelling. The conquest had destroyed the O.E. literary standard,
and when the native literature emerged again, each writer
established his own standard. This lack of a standard dialect
combined with dialectal variations, new French words and
traditional O.E. spellings made a uniform mode practically
impossible until printing came.

(9)   <u>The most important orthographic variations among the vowel</u>

It is important to note that, where there has been a
sound change, either in vowels or consonants, the old symbol
and the one representing the new sound will overlap. Hence, a̲e̲
is commonly found in M.E. beside the a̲ or o̲ which describe
the O.E. sounds.

The symbols most to be noted among the vowels are
those in connection with a͞e͞, c̄, ɛ̄, ō̲, ŭ nd y̆. ǣ disappeared
entirely during the O.E. period, though they were frequently
interchanged ith e͞a͞ in M.E.; ē (e:) as spelled i̲e̲ during
the greater part of the period, though e̲e̲ was introduced in
L.M.E.; e (ɛ) was spelled a̲e̲, e̲, e̲a̲ in M.E. and e̲e̲ for
th rest of the period; ō̲ -(ɔ·) as written o̲a̲ an

indication of the open quality of the vowel, or oo as an
indication of its length; ŭ appeared as ŏ next the letters
m,n,y , to avoid confusion; ū became generally written ou;
O.E. ў as written u; and ȳ was written ui. For a detailed
survey of all the vowel symbols, see the Orthographic Chart in
the appendix,

(9.I) ae *14) It is generally agreed that ǽ underwent
phonetic change in M.E., and both the sounds and the symbols
are different, although in M.E. texts the ae symbol does
survive until the beginning of the 13th century, especially in
the South.

    However, in I.O.E. and L.W.E. ǽhe ǽ were represented
by either ae or ea, for, during this period ǽa had smoothed
to ǽ, although they were still written ǽu. The ea spelling
for ę̄ survives the M.E. period in Anglo-Norman texts, and in
early modern English (the 15th and 16th centuries) this symbol
is re-adopted into English texts for the ę̄ sound. *15. e.g.-
hāl lan - E.M.E. spelled haelen/healen - W.E., helen (ę̄)(hɛːlən)
The ea reappears later, borrowed from Anglo-Norman texts in
modern heal.

(9.2) ē (e:) This e was commonly spelled ie in E.E., but in
L.M.E. the ie was almost ousted in favour of ee. The ie spelling
was still found, most often in words of Anglo-Norman origin
since this was the French spelling for ē.(e:) *16 It was also
frequent in L.E. owing to Anglo-Norman influence, and to the

fact that, in M.t., ē came from īo which developed in E.M.E. to
.t. īe. This īe became ę though the ie symbol was still used
after the development. In E.M.E. the ie symbol was freely
adopted for ē in words of any origin - e.g. field, chief, etc.
(9.3) ǭ (ɔ:) In many instances in M.E. ǭ arose from O.L. ā.
There was no regular mode of spelling this sound in M.E., but
two methods have survived. In S. . there was a tendency to
differentiate between ǭ and ọ̄ by spelling the first oa. This
This spelling appears in many modern words - boat, coat, etc.
Another mode appeared in M.E. in the first half of the 14th
century in the spelling oo. However, though this indicates length,
it does not differentiate between ǭ and ọ̄.
(9.4) ŭ In M.E., u was written o from about 1250 on, especially
before letters such as m,n,v,w, where confusion might arise.
Occasionally in other positions, u was written o since the sound
in Anglo-Norman was represented by the o symbol. o for u was not
so common north of the Humber.[17]
(9.5) ū From about 1230, there appears an ou spelling for ū. [18]
There are two reasons for the adoption of this symbol - (a) the ou
symbol was used in Anglo-Norman texts for ū (u:) (b) It was
necessary to differentiate between long back ū (u:) and long
front rounded ü (Y:) which was also written u in E.M.E.
However, the ou spelling does not indicate any change in pronunciation of ū.
e.g. O.E. tūn is spelled toun in M.E., but there is no difference
in pronunciation.

(9.6) $\bar{\bar{y}}$ In O.E. the sounds of (y) and (y:) were represented
by the $\bar{y}$ symbol. In M.E., this sound only survives in the S...
dialect, and here, from the 13th century on, the symbol u was
substituted for y since the sound corresponded to French u
(written u). As a result, it became necessary to distinguish
between long (y:) and short (y). Short (y) was still written u,
but ui was used for long (y:)   *19
e.g. C.E. brȳd was written brud, bruid, bruyd in M.E.   This
symbol only survives today in bruise (O.E. brȳsan) and build
(C.E. byldan).

Although the y symbol was no longer used for front rounded
u in M.E., it came to be used quite early as a variant of I. At
first, it was used for i next to the letters m,n,v,w with which
i might be confused, but later i and y were used interchangeably
regardless of the neighboring consonant. This practice became
more regular owing to the fact that in the Mid. and Nth.
dialects, the sound of y itself had changed to i, but for some
time after the change, the y symbol was used.

(10)   The chief orthographic changes in the consonants.

The most interesting orthographic developments in
the consonants are in connection with c, ȝ, h, f,ƀ,ð, s, runic w
and the groups sc, cw and hw.

The first three are the most intricate, for, in ...
they each had two or more sound values expressed by one symbol.
... c represented two sounds, front c (tʃ), and back c (k).

In M.E. the first came to be written ch, or when doubled, cch;
the second was written either c or k.   O.E. ʒ came to be
written with the continental g symbol everywhere except where
it was a front continuant (j).   Here, the O.E. symbol was retained,
though y was used in later M.E.   The two sounds for h were that
of the usual aspirate (h) and that of a voiceless continuant (χ)
(Scot. loch).   The first has always been expressed by the
letter h, but in M.E. the second was written h, ʒ, , ʒh and later
ch or gh in Low. Scot.

In O.E. f, and s had voiced and voiceless qualities
which were given different symbols in M.E.   The voiced f was
written v; voiced s was written z in some dialects, while voiceless s was written either s or c.

The O.E. symbols, þ (θ) and ð (ð), disappeared altogether
during the M.E. period and their place was taken by th which
was used for both sounds.   Runic w, which was used throughout
O.E. texts, was entirely ousted in favor of the continental w
symbol.

SC was written ss or s in E.M.E. generally, and this
was retained throughout the period of Kt.   Elsewhere, the sh
writing was used.   The sound cw (kw) was written as qu very
early in M.E. and this spelling was general by the end of the
13th century.   hw was written wh uniformly by the early 14th
century except north of the Humber where the sound had changed.
Here cuh is found.

(1)   (11)
(10.1) c O.E. c represented two sounds—front c(tʃ), and back to c (k).

(1) In early M.E. French scribes began to use ch for this sound since it was the Anglo-N. symbol for (tʃ), —A.-N. chambre. Where the c was geminated, sometimes chch is found (e.g. Ayenbite of Inwit), but more usually cch was used and later the double c simplified. [20]

e.g. O.E. wrecca M.E.(wretʃə) written in M.E. wrecche, wreche, and rarely wrechche.

(11) In M.L. back c was written k except when it occurred before a back vowel. In this position, the c symbol is retained. [20]

e.g. O.E. boc—M.E. bok, but O.E. cae lf appears in M.E. as calf. Geminated back c was at first written kk, but towards the end of the M.E. period, the symbol ck was adopted, e.g. O.E. bucc—M.E. bukk—buck.

(10.2) ʒ [21] In all positions except here ʒ was a front continuant, the O.E. symbol was replaced by the continental g. Where it was a front continuant (j), the O.E. symbol was retained sporadically to the end of the period, although from the beginning of the 14th century on, it was replaced by y but even this was not uniform.

e.g. O.E. doʒʒ a —written in M.E. dogge
      "   bricʒ   "   "   " brigge
but   '   ʒift   "   M.M.L.   ʒift, later yift.

[22]
(10.3) h   In O.   ther   was a two sounds initial aspirate

aspirate is still written <u>h</u>, but the other sound differs. Even at the end of the O.E. period, voiceless <u>h</u> might be written h or ʒ since, in L.O.E., final back continuant ʒ had unvoiced to <u>h</u> but was still often written ʒ . Hence, the two symbols became interchan\geable. In E.M.E. came the adoption of both symbols together to express the voiceless continuant <u>h</u>. Later, not commonly until the 14th century, the continuant ʒ symbol was replaced by the continental g, and so <u>gh</u> became another variant. In Low. Scot. <u>ch</u> was adopted for the <u>h</u> (X) sound, Thus, O.E. cniht appears in M.E. as kniht, kniʒt, kniʒht, and Scot. knicht.

(10.4) <u>f</u> The two sounds that this letter stood for in O.E. were a voiceless continuant (f) and its voiced equivalent (v) sound-ho<u>f</u> (voiceless), ha<u>f</u>ast (voiced). In order to distinguish them, the French scribes of the M.E. period adopted <u>v</u> altogether for the voiced sound, though it is true that the <u>v</u> can be found in L.O.E. O.E. <u>hafast</u> appears in M.E. as <u>havest</u>.

(10.5) <u>s</u> It is in only a few of the southern dialects, and notably Kt. that any difference is found in writing voiced <u>s</u> (z) and voiceless <u>s</u>.(S) However, in these districts, the voiced sound is spelled <u>z</u>. There is a new writing for voiceless <u>s</u> to be found beside the old one. In A.-N., the voiceless <u>s</u> was frequently expressed by <u>c</u> before e or i. Therefore, <u>c</u> with e or i had the <u>s</u> sound. Some confusion resulted in M.E. when the <u>c</u> symbol was adopted into native ords.

Where s should have survived, sometimes c is found. O.L. mȳs
should give M.E. mīs, but mice is found instead.

(10.6) ƀ and ð.[23] In O.E. these symbols were used indiscrim-
inately for the voiced (ð) and voiceless (Ɵ) th sound.
Early in M.E., ð began to disappear and it was gone entirely
early in the 14th century. ƀ remained in fairly regular use
until the end of the 14th century, but, beside this, very
generally in the second half of the 14th century, the th symbol
of uncertain origin was used.

(10.7) sc In O.E. this sound probably was explosive -(sk),
but during the O.E. period, the sound was modified so that by
the end of the 11th century, - some scholars say much earlier ,-[24]
it had developed into a pure sibilant (ʃ). Therefore, French
scribes wrote it at first as ss or s, and this writing was
retained in Kt. throughout the period. Elsewhere, the later
mode of writing it as sh (probably on the analogy of ch for c)
ousted the ss/s writing. An sch writing is found most commonly
in Low. Scot., but also in Southern.
O.E. scip appears in M.E. as ssip/sip (retained in Kt.) ship,
schip.

(10.8) cw (kw) Very early in M.E. the French scribes began to
use their symbol qu for this sound. Both symbols are found
in the Peterborough Chronicle, but qu soon ousts cw. Hence, O.E.
cwen is written quen in M.E.

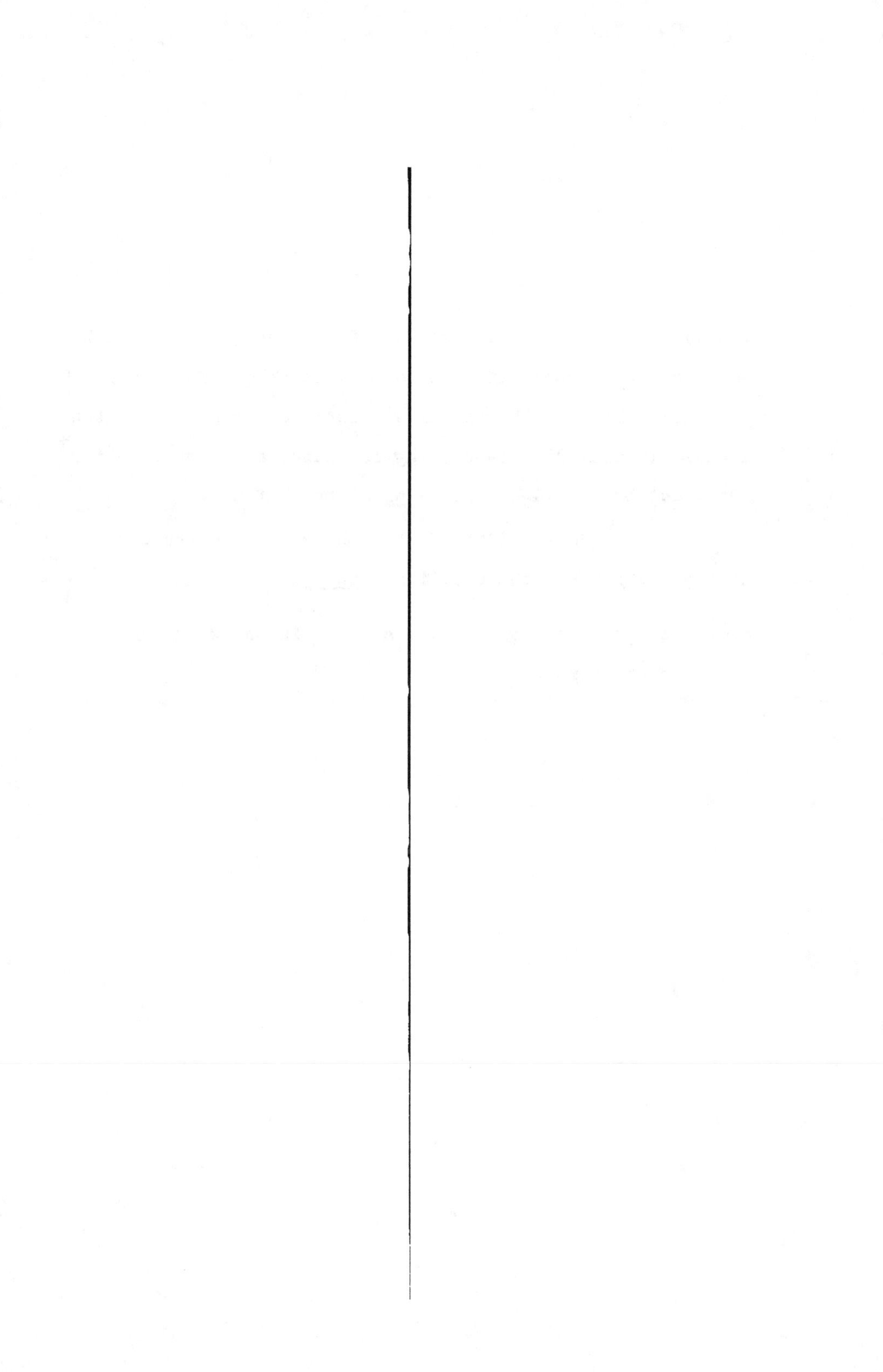

(10.9) <u>hw</u>   Although the sound did not change in the dialec
south of the Humber, it came to be written <u>wh</u>, for the scrib
probably felt that the labial element was the more important
sound. In the 13th century, <u>hw</u> is found; both occur in the
13th; but by the 14th century <u>wh</u> alone is found. [29]

North of the Humber, however, the sound chang
to (kw), which was there written <u>quh.</u>

e.g. O.E. <u>hwil</u> appears in M.E. as <u>whil</u> in the south and
<u>quhil</u> in the north.

CHRONOLOGICAL CHANGES IN CONSONANTS

	11th	12th	12th	14th
c (front) (t∫) (back) (k)	o c/k	c/ch c/k	ch k/o	ch k/o
ȝ (usual) (g) (ft. cont.) (j)	ȝ ȝ	ȝ/g ȝ	g ȝ	g ȝ/y (more often)
h (cont.) (X)	h/ȝ	h/ȝ/ȝh	h/ȝ/ȝh/gh	ch/ch (Low. Scot.)
f (voiced) (v)	f/v(rare)	f/v	v	v
s (voiced) (z) (voice- less) (s)	s s	s/z (Kt.) s	s/z s/c	s/z s/c
đ (ð)	đ	đ (occas.)	th	th
þ (θ)	þ	þ	þ/th (rare)	th/þ (rare)
sc (∫)	sc	sc//ss/s (remain in Kt.)	sh	sh/sch (Low. Scot.)
cw (kw)	cw	cw/qu	qu	qu
hw (hw)	hw	hw	hw/wh	wh/quh (Low. Scot)

CHAPTER V

Phonology: Sound Changes - Lengthening and Shortening

(12)   Sound Changes. The sound changes in '. E. are
primarily concerned with the vowels, and may be considered
under two headings: (1) Quantitative and (2) Qualitative
changes.

uentitative changes deal with the len th of the
vowels, and may again be divided into (A) Shortening and
(B) lengthening. There are evidences of both in the '.E.
period, and they occur more or less continuously throughout
the M.E. period. They are common to all dialects.

(13)   Shortening. *25

The shortening of O.E. long vowels occurred under
several conditions:

before two consonants

in the first elements of compounds

in the first syllable of a trisyllabic word

in unstressed words or syllables.

(13 1) The shortening of long vowels before two consonants
began about the end of the 10th century and the beginning of
the 11th.

Hence, older clädd became M.E. clăd

'   söfte   '   '   sŏrt

'   t ŏntiʒ   '   '   t ŏtt1

'   li fʒ   '   "   blĭss

ases - þīones (gen.) - has disappeared

the nominative has been levelled into a

und, O.E. lȳtel should keep the long v

vowel of the oblique cases has been lev

'little', from O.E. lȳtle (dat.) result

(13.2) The shortening of the first el

occurred to some extent in L.O.E.

O.E. wīsdōm became L.O.E. is

beside this is the long vowel surviving

E. hūswīf from O.E. hūswīf beside the

vowels in M.E. 'house' and 'life'

(13.5) Apparently there were two peri

first syllable of a trisyllabic word.

O.E. and the other in the M.E. period.

are frequently two distinct forms for t

wīsdōmȝ. by the first shortening bec

hich survives in the M.E. proper na e

hālidaeȝ became O.E. hōlidæȝ which became M.E. hōl[i]
and then through shortening gave M.E. hōliday.
13.4) The vowels of many unstressed words such as t[he]
article - ān - and some pronouns such as 'ūs' were sh[ortened]
Other unstressed syllables were also shortened, notab[ly]
a) the second elements of compounds - see huswif and
b) many suffixes in place names- tūn, bȳ, hām, lēa -
Kingestūn and hitbȳ from O.E. Cynestūn and Hwītbȳ.
14) Lengthening. *27 Lengthening of a short vo[wel]
in M.E. when the vowel was in an open, accented sylla[ble]
are two divisions in lengthening according to time:

    (1) the vowels a,o,e.

    (11) the vowels i,u.

14.1) The vowels a,o,e, apparently underwent lengt[hening]
during the 12th century in the north and during the l[ater]
in the south.

    a. scămu -- O.E. shăme -- shāme (12th cent. 13th
        făeder --Nth.Mid. făder - fāder 13th (develo[p]
                M.E. ā survives in Irish 'fay
        ĕalu --ăelu--Nth.Mid. ăle -- āle 13th.

    o nŏsu --nŏse --nōse (n ɔːz ə)
        ꝼŏtu --thrŏte --thrōte. (θr ɔːt ə)

    e stĕlan --stĕlĕn--stōlen (stɛːʃən) M.E. steal
        nĕodu --nĕde (Nth.,W.Mid.,..t.) nōde(M.E:mɛːdə).

27

(14.2)   The vowels <u>i,u</u>, lengthened during the 13th century
in the North, and during the 14th in the South. This lengthening was less uniform than the <u>a,o,e</u> one, and was frequently
obscured by further changes and by analogy with unlengthened
forms.

<u>i</u> After <u>i</u> lengthened, the long <u>i</u> in turn became e (e:)
The lengthening here occurred more regularly in the north than
in the south, but even then there was a tendency to adopt
short vowels from adjacent dialectal forms.

    <u>i</u>   O.E. wĭcu--".E. wīke--wēke (we:kə)--N.E. .eck

       O.E. bĭtol--".E.bītel--bētel(be:tə{)--N.E.beetle

       O.E. ўfel--".E.īvel--ēvel--N.E. evil.

<u>u</u> The lengthening of short <u>u</u> was less common than that
of short <u>i</u>. Here, again, the lengthened vowel underwent a
further change: ū became ō.(o:)

       O.E. dŭru--".E. dūre--dōre (do:rə)--N.E. ᴅoor

       O.E. wŭdu--".E. wūde--wōde--N.E. wood

(15) <u>Variations due to lengthening.</u> In closely related forms,
the conditions for lengthening were often present in one while
lacking in another. The result was that this variation le to
the construction of new forms through analogy. The effects are
most clearly seen in three places:

    (1) in monosyllabic nouns and adjectives

    (2) in disyllabic nouns and adj ctives.

    (3) in auxiliary verb forms.

28

(15.1) <u>In monosyllabic nouns and adjectives</u>, there was
considerable cross-levelling, the results of hich can be seen
in modern forms.

```
long vowel   ) O.L. hwăc l--!'.E. whăl--  N.L.whale (vowel from
levelled     ) inflected cases)  hwăe les-- .'.E.whāles
             )
short vowel  ) O.L. păcf --!'.E. păth--N.E. path
levelled.    )      păcfes      pāthes  (disappeared)
             )
both vowels  ) O.L. stăe f--!'.L.  stăff--N.L. staff
retained     )      stăe fes       stāves       staves.
```

(15.2) <u>Disyllabic nouns and adjectives</u> show the s me levelling.

```
short vowel  ) O.L.  sădol--!'.L. sādel  (disappeared)
levelled     )       sădoles      săd(e)les--N.E. saddle's
             )                    (levelled into ron.)
             )
long vowel   ) O.L. crădol--!'.E. crādel--N.E. cradle.
levelled     )      crădoles-      crăd(e)les  (disappeared),
             )
             )
Both vowels)
retained     ) O.L. gămen--N.E. game    O.E. scŏadu-- N.E. shade
with differ-}
ing meaning ) O.E. gămenes--N.E. gammon O.E. scŭd.es--N.E.shadow
```

(15.3) <u>In auxiliary verb forms</u>, there were frequently variations
according as the word received more or less stress. Thus, in '.E.
the forms <u>ăren</u> and <u>āren</u> occurred side by side, though the form
with the long vowel has ince disappeared. Likewise, <u>hăven</u> and
<u>hāven</u> occurred. The '.L. auxiliary 'have' comes from the form
with the short vowel, but the long vowel survives in a derived
word 'behave'.

Qualitative Sound Changes: O.E. Simple

16) Qualitative changes. These changes tr
f O.E. simple vowels and diphthongs; of th
n N.E., and of certain miscellaneous conso
17) O.E. Simple Vowels. In treating of O
ecessary to make two divisions: (1) the vo
emained unchanged in M.E., and (ii) those

(i) Those vowels which normally remai
re: short a, long e(e:), short e, long and
∂), long and short u.   hen conditions
hortening were present, of course, these v
ccordingly. [28]

(ii) The vowels which had peculiar dev
hort ae, long ae (æ :) long a, long o (o:)

18) Variation in Normally Unchanged Vowel

Even the vowels which normally remai
ometimes influenced by neighboring consona
sually took place in connection with n or
18.1) ă/ŏ plus nasal. [29] Apparently, in th
f O.E., ă plus a nasal rounded to a sound
a and ∂).   During the O.E. period, the t

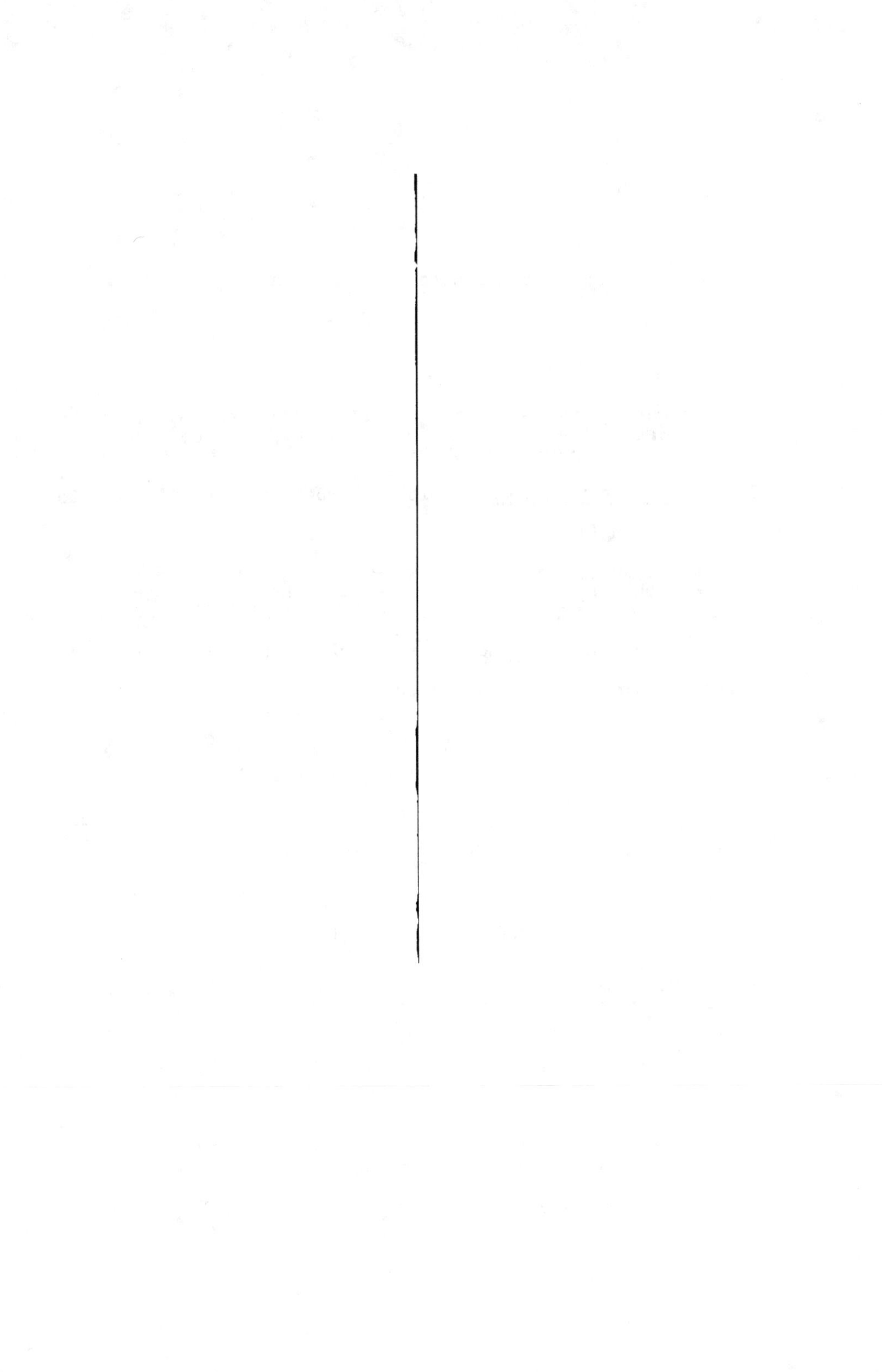

occasionally found in all dialects, the normal type for
'.Mid. was the _o_ type, while in the Nth., S.., and Kt. dialects,
the normal type was _a_.

'.E. mann(man)   ----M.E. man   all dialects except '.Mid.
    monn (mɔn)   ----M.E. mon(mɔn) '.Mid., but not
                uniform in S.".Mid.
(18.2)   Raising of ĕ to ĭ. This was probably a normal phonetic
change before ng(ŋ).

..E. seng(e)an (seŋ gan)   --'.E. singe(siŋgə)
      heng (heŋ)   --M.E. henge (heŋgə)
      Englisc (eŋgliʃ)   --M.E. Inglish (iŋgliʃ)

        The raising of _e_ to _i_ before _nch_ may possibly have been
a phonetic chan e in some areas in L."... *30

O.E. stenc(stentʃ) --M.E. stench(stentʃ) --stynch (stintʃ),
                found in Trevisa, S.".Mid., late 14th.

        here forms with _i_ occur in ".M.E., they can usually be
explained by anal gy with closely related forms.
    e.g. ʃ inchen beside ʃ enchen, from .E. ʃenc(e)an _may_ be due
    to analogy with O.E. ʃync(e) an   (to seem).

(18.3) Long or short i preceded by w. Apparently, already in
L.O.E., _wi_ sometimes rounded to _wy_, so that, in the ". . and
'.Mid. districts where y usually preserved the rounded value-
written _u_-there are _wu_ (wy) forms beside _wi_ forms.
    O... wiste--L. .E. wyste/wiste--- .. wiste(wistə) 'erido
            occasional writing wuste(wystə) in ". . and . id
    O.E, wīfman--L.O.". wīmman/wymman--'. . wīm an/wūmman (wmn)ʳ
                     wūm on(wynɔn) '. id.

A writing woman also occurs in W.S.,
indicating a retracting of this wu to wu,
since o would not be written for u(y)
although u was often so written next to
m,n,v,w,

(10) Vowels which did change in M.E.

The development of the vowels [*31]$\breve{ae},\bar{a},\bar{o}$ and $\bar{y}$ [*32]
varies considerably in different districts in M.E.   It is to
these vowels, therefore, that we look for the divergencies
which constitute dialectal characteristics.

(10.1) Development in the Nth. dialect. [*33]

$\breve{ae}$--$\breve{a}$ In the very early M.E. or late O.E. $\breve{ae}$ retracted to $\breve{a}$.

O.E. wæs s (wæs)--M.E. was (was)

Occasionally, o is found where a is expected. This has
been explained as the result of (a) the influence
candinavian cognates, and (b) the weakening of the vowel in
unstressed positions.

        (a) efter for after -- cp. O.N. optir
        (b) Wes for was in unstressed positions.

$\bar{ae}$--$\bar{e}$.
(æ: > ε·)   O.E. Long ae from whatever source becomes long, open
            e in Nth.

            O.E. clæc ne(kl æ :ne)-- M.E. clene(kl ε :n∂)

$\bar{a}$--$\bar{a}$--$\bar{o}$?
(a:- ε :)   O.E. long a remained unchanged in Nth. in E.M.E.,
            although evidence of rhyme in the 14th century suggests
            that, by that time, a had fronted to ae (æ :), and
            possibly had been raised to e(ε :).   The a spelling
            survived throughout the period, but from the second

half of the 14th century on, ai/ay were com on writings for
a especially in Low. Scot.

O.N. nāra --W.M. Nth. nāre(na:rə)--nāe re(næ:rə ?
--more(nɛ:rə) written ai/ay.

__ō--ū__
(o: > y:)

From the late 13th century on, o appears to have been
raised and rounded to ū(y:), which was identifie with
French u. The sound is spelled variously o/u/ui/uy.

O.E. gōd(go:d) --W.M. Nth. gūd(gy:d), written god, gud,
guid, guyd.

__y̆--ĭ__
(y, ι)
(y·, ι·)

Very early, possibly already in L.O.E., y, long and short
front rounded u, unround to i in Nth.

O.E. bry̆cg   --Nth.(early) brĭcg.

(19.2) Developments in the W.Mid. dialect.   *35

__ăe--ă__

As in Nth., O.E. ăe early retracted to ă.
O.E. stae f -- W.Mid. staff.

__āe--ō__
(æ: > ɛ:)

The development of āe also follows W.M., to long
open e,

ee̸

O.E. hāe lan(hae:lan)-- W.Mid. hēlen (hɛ:lən)

__ā--ō__
(a:-ɔ:)
ɔ.

This change constitutes one of the most important
differences between Nth. and the southern dialects. O..ā
became ō in all dialects south of the Humber. his change is
evidenced in W.Mid. as early as the middle of the 12th century
in the Peterborough Chronicle. It was general by the en of
the first quarter of the 13th century.

ō--ō O.E. o remained unchanged, although occasionally, in the
14th century, an __ou__ spelling is found for ō. This has led
scholars to postulate the raising of ō to ū, but nothing
definite has been decided. Moreover, see Wyld, section 163.

  O.E. sōna --M.E. sōno, south of the Humber

y̆--ĭ. Again, W.Mid. follows Nth. in the change of y to i.

  O.E. cynn(kyn) --N.E., W.Mid. kĭn.

  So far, then, the only difference between Nth. and W.Mid.
has been in the development of ā to ō.

(19.3) __Developments in W.Mid.__*36

ăe--ă O.E. __ae__ became __a__ in W.Mid. also, although there were
occasional e types up to the first quarter of the 14th century
in parts of W.Mid.

  O.E. făe der-- W.Mid. făder (early fęder)

āe--ē W.Mid. follows the development in Nth. and E.Mid. for long ae.
(æ: > ɛ.)

  O.E. dāe lan --W.Mid. dēlen.

ā--ō. In common with the other dialects south of the Humber, W.Mid.
(a:-ɔ:)
has the development of ā to ō.

  O.E. stān--W.M. (south of the Humber) stōne(stɔ:nə)

ū--ō Here, also, the W.Mid. development agrees with that of other
(o:-o:)
southern dialects. For all practical purposes, O.E. ō
remained south of the Humber in M.E.

  O.E. fōs --W.M.(south of the Humber) fōs (fo:s)

y̆--y̆. The O.E. y had a sound resembling that of French u-i.e. a
front rounded u sound. In W.Mid., this rounded value survives
throughout the period as the normal sound for O.E. y. It fell in

wit' the French u, and therefore can be written, as early

as the 12th century, **u** or, in the case of the long vowel, **ui**.

O.E. brȳd --- .'id. brūde(bry:d), wr t'en brude or bruide)

T'e only extensive difference between ..'id. and '.'id. in

t'e developme t of simple vowels is this one of O.E. y.

Isewhere, the two dialects a ree, and have the same points of

difference (the developments of long $\bar{a}$ and of long $\bar{o}$) with the

'th.

(19.4) Developments in B.'.   *37

$\frac{\breve{ae}-\breve{e}}{\text{ousted b-}}$
'id.a   '.E. ae appears to have been raised, in early transition-

al '.E., to '.E. e, which was written ae,e and (rarely) ea.

This is the most remarkable difference between '.E. and the

dialects to the north.

However, the 'id. a type began to encroach upon '.E. e

as early as the 12th century, and, by the 14th century 'ad

ousted t'e e type entirely.

O.E. cræ ft --'.E. creft(early), ousted by 'id.craft.

$\frac{\bar{ae}-\bar{e}}{(\text{æ}:-\text{ɛ}:)}$ O.E. long ae from whatever source became lon open e in

'.E. as in 'id. and Nth.

O.E. '.E. dǣ d(d æ :d) --H.E. ... dēd (dɛ :d)

$\frac{\bar{a}-\bar{o}}{(\text{a}:-\text{ɔ}:)}$ '.E. follows the usual southern development of $\bar{a}$ to $\bar{o}$.

O.E. bāt --'...(---t' t e Hun'er) bōt (bɔ :t)

N... boat.

$\bar{o}-\bar{o}$ O.E. ō remains in ... ... as o. Occasi nally i' is

s elled **ou**.

O.'. bōc -- .. bōk ... boo'.

$\breve{\bar{y}}-\breve{\bar{y}}$.   'ere, t e ...develop ent a re s it t a' of .'id.

in retaining the rounde value of O... y.

35

O.E. fȳr -- M.E. fūr(fy:r)

The developments in S.E. agree with those of W.Mid. except for that of short ae becoming short o

(19.5) <u>Developments in Kentish.</u> [*38]

ăĕ--ŏ.   Already in O.E. inthe 9th century, aĕ had been raised to ŏ in Kt. Unlike the S. . ŏ, the Kt. ŏ held its own beside the Mid. ă to the end f the M. .period.

O.E. þac t --O.E. 9th c.   þet--M.E. Kt. thet.

āĕ -L.O.E.ō. Already in L.O.E., early O.E. āĕ from any source had
<u>(æ :--o:)</u> become Kt. long e. This e became M.E. Kt. long, close e(e:). It was spelled variously e/ie/ye throughout the period.

O.E. slāĕ pan-- O.E. Kt. slōpan--M.E. Kt. slōpen(sle:p ə n)

a--o   Kt. has the regular southern development of ā to ō.
<u>(a:-- ə :)</u>
O.E. bān --M.E. southern bōne (b ə :n ə)

ŏ-- ō   Here, again, Kt. has the usual southern retension of o, spelled occasionally <u>ou</u>.

O.E. nōna   --M.E. southern nōne(mo:n ə)

ȳ-L.O.E. ĕ. This is a distinctive mark of the Kentish dialect. Lead-
<u>(y -- e)</u> in O.E. in the Kentish area, ȳ had unrounded and lowered to ĕ. Tus occurred possibly as early as the 9th century,although e spelling does not become common until the 10th century. The e persisted throughout the M. . peri d.

O.E. myriʒ --L.O.E. Kt. meriʒ (meri ʒ)--M.E. Kt. merie (meri ə).

The differences between Kt. and W. .le in the develop-ments of O. . āĕ, a d O. . ȳ. Then, too, t Kt. development

of aĕ to ŏ was much earlier than that of W.., and it
survived throughout the M.E. period.

(20) By way of grouping the dialectal developments, one may
say that W.Mid. agrees with Nth. in the developments of long
and short ae, and long and short y. E.Mid. and all other
dialects differ from Nth. in the developments of $\bar{a}$ and $\bar{o}$.

        Since $\bar{a}$ and $\bar{o}$ had common developments south of the
Humber, the only vowels left to show variation there are aĕ
and $\breve{\bar{y}}$. E.Mid., in the change of y to i differs from W.Mid.,
which agrees with S.W. in its treatment of y. In the single
vowels, the only divergence of S.W. from W.Mid. is that of
aĕ becoming ŏ, and even this occurs occasionally in W.Mid.

        Kentish shows the widest divergence from the other
southern dialects in that aĕ becomes ĕ and is not ousted by
ă; and $\breve{\bar{y}}$ have a peculiar development to ĕ.

(21) The vowels that show variations in W.., therefore, have
the following forms:

O...		Transition	S.W.
short ae(ae)	Nth.	a	a
	E.Mid.	a	a
	W.Mid.	a/e	a/e (some beginning of 14th century)
	S.W.	o	e (ousted by a in 14th century)
e 9th. Kt.		o	e (occasional a forms)

Conclusion: a predominates by beginning of 14th except in Kt.

O.E.		Transition	M.E.
Long ae (æ:)	Nth.	long, open	e(ɛ:)
	E.Mid.	" "	"
	W.Mid.	" "	"
	S.W.	" "	"
ē	Kt.	long, close	e(e:)

Conclusion: O.E. æ became long, open e except in Kt.

where it had already become e in O.E.

Long a(a:)			
	Nth.	ā	ā
	E. Mid.	ō (ə :)	ō
	W. Mid.	o	"
	S.W.	o	"
	Kt.	o	"

Conclusion: ā remained in Nth.; elsewhere it became (ə:) .

long o (o:)			
	Nth.	ō	u(y:) late 13th.
	E.Mid.	ō	o(o:) 14th, spelled ou
	W.Mid.	"	"
	S.W.	"	"
	Kt.	"	"

Conclusion: long o was raised and rounded to u(y:) in Nth.

Elsewhere, it remained in W.S. as long, close o

long and			
short y (y)	Nth.	i	i
	E. Mid.	i	i
	W.Mid.	u(y)	u
	S.W.	"	"
e 9th	Kt.	e	e

Conclusion: y shows the greatest variation of any vowel. Nth.

and E.Mid. unround to i; W.Mid. and S.W. keep the

rounded u value; and Kt. u rounds and lowers to e,

The O.E. diphthongs were: long and short ea (æ:ə
                         long and short eo (o:o,
                         long and short io (i:o,
                         long and short ie (&

                              (i:ə , and iə)

          The general line of development of these di
ample. All O.E. diphthongs underwent monophthongiz
.   Probably the tendency was already becoming gene
., although the traditional diphthongic symbols wer
ally used in writing and, indeed, survive well on i
period in some dialectal areas.   *39

long and short ea *40 smoothed to long and short ae
O.E. since there are occasional ae spellings in L.O
. i.e.-(æ:ə) became simply (æ :), and (eo ə)

long and short eo *41 smoothed to long and short fro
ing the 10th century. That is, (o:o) became (ö), a
o (ö).   The smoothing was probably complete by the
e century. (In some areas of the 9th and . ld., o
ve smoothed directly to e very early. Evidence can
 in the Peterborough Chronicle of the first half o
century.)

long and short io *42 had become eo in all dialects o

early enough in O.E. to fall in with the regular
developments of ēo. In Kt., it became īe in ..E. .

Short io fell in with ōo during the O.E. period except
in Nth.   Here, the io smoothed to short i.

(22.1) The peculiarity in Kentish diphthongs.*45 Whereas, in all
other dialects, the smoothing of the diphthongs seems to indicate
that the first element was the stronger, in Kt., it would seem
that the second element was the more definite. The spelling of
Kt. diphthongs supports this assumption. For instance, the
spellings ea, _ia_ _ye_ and _ya_ for the Kt. ēa diphthong indicate
that the first vowel of the diphthong is the indeterminate one,
while the second retains its full vowel value, though the
sound may be changed. Therefore, it is said that Kt. diphthongs
show _shifted_ _stress_ from the normal position on the first element,
to the second. Such diphthongs as the Kt. are called _rising_
diphthongs since the stress increases in the second element,
while other diphthongs, showing decreasing stress, are called
falling diphthongs.

(23) _Dialectal_ _developments_ _of_ _O.E._ _diphthongs._

Apart from the Kt. developments, O.E. diphthongs
underwent the common change of smoothing to monophthongs. To
this point, however, they developed as did the simple vowels in
the various dialects.

(23.1) _Northern_

Short ea, having smoothed to short ae, developed as did
original short ae to short a.

ēa--ă
(aoə -a)

40

O.E. eart ---L.O.E. ae rt --W.E. Wth. art
(ae ə rt)---- (ae rt) (art)

ēa --ē̄
(æə --Ɛ:)

Long ea(æ :ə), having smoothed to long ae (æ :), became long, open e (Ɛ :)

O.E. dēaþ (dæ :əϴ) -- L.O.E. dēoþ (dæ :ϴ) --W.E. deth (d Ɛ :ϴ)

ĕo --ŏ̆
(eo--e)

Short eo (eo), having smoothed to front rounded (ø) unrounded to (e).

O.E. heorte -- L.O.E. heorte --- W.E. (12th) hø̜rte) - Wth. herte.

ēo --ō̄
(e:o--e:)

Long eo had the same development as short eo in Wth. It smoothed to long, close e,

O.L. dēop --- L.O.E. dēop -- W.E. (12th) - (dø:p) -- Wth. dōp (do:p)

ĭo --ĭ.
(io-- i)

Long io became long eo in O.E., and had the same development, but the short diphthong remained in Wth and smoothed to ĭ in W.E.

O.E. miol(u)c -- W.E. Wth. milk.

(X.2) West Midland.

The developments here were practically the same as those for Wth. The only difference in the two dialects is that usually, O.E. ĭo had become ōo in the O.E. period, although there are a few instances of the io retained and smoothed to ĭ in WMid.

41

(32.3) <u>West Midland</u>.

Long and short ea had the same developments as in
Nth., but long and short eo differed. Instead of unrounding
to $\bar{\breve{o}}$ after smoothing to (ø: and ø), they retained the rounded
value throughout the whole of the W.M. period. The sound was,
at first, very generally written eo, and the diphthongic
writing survives in some areas of W.Mid. as late as the 14th
century, but very early the spellings ue, oe, o, iu,u begin
to be found. Of these, the <u>u</u> spelling is by far the most
frequent (through the influence of Anglo-Norman orthography).

    O.E. corʃe (coreʒe)-- E.M. (12th) (øre) and remains
                                                       in W.Mid.
    O.E. ʃeof (eo:of) --E.M. (12th) (eø:f) and remains in
        W.Mid.   spelled ʃeof, ʃuef, ʃuf, etc.

(33.4) <u>South Western</u>

Short ea, after smoothing to short ae, became short o
(see W.M. simple vowels). However, as in the case of original
ae, the e was ousted by the Mid. a by the beginning of the
14th century.

    O.E. sceadu --E.M.E. sceadu(ʃac du) -- W.M.E.
        shedwe(ʃodwe) which was ousted by shadwe.

Long ae followed the change in the other dialects.

Long and short eo took the same form in S.W. as in W.M.:
they remained at the rounded o (ø: and ø) sound throughout
the period.

42

O.E., deore (de:ork) -- M.E. (15th)   (dø:rk),
which remained in S.E., writ en deork, duerk, dork, durk.
                                       c   o   o   c

ie--i/y.
(ie--i/y)

One of the most important characteristics of the
S.E. dialect was the ie diphthong.

ie(i:ə) had already smoothed before the end of the
O.E. period. There were two different periods of smoothing.
The first was during the 9th century, when long and short
ie smoothed to long and short i in some areas of Essex.
There, however, the diphthong survived this, it underwent a
later smoothing and rounding to (y: and y).

Both the (i) and the (y) forms survived throughout the
M.E. period in S.E., though the (y) forms came to be spelled
u from the early 14th century on.

O.E. W.S. hierde--9th hirde --L.O.E. hirde --S.(hirdə)
               hierde   (hyrde)   (hyrdə)

(23.5) Kentish.

ea --a.
(æəᵃ --a)

In Kt., there was an unusual development of short ea
to short a. Apparently, the Kt. raising of ǣ to ē, which
occurred in the 9th century, was earlier than the smoothing
of ea to æ. Therefore, the æ arising from this later
source was not affected by the raising and simply retracted
in L.O.E. to ā.

O.E. Kt. (hæᵃlf)--L.Kt. hælf(hælf) -- M.E.
Kt. half(half).

The development of ēa in Kt. is doubtful, but the

ēa--ē
(æə -- ɛ:)

spellings yea, ya, ia. ye. ie, in M.E. suggests that this diphthong did not smooth as soon as the same diphthong in other dialects, and they also suggest that there was a shifting od stress from the first to the second element. This element would then have been fronted and raised to e, and the first element would gradually have disappeared.

i.e. O.E. Kt. ēa --L.O.E. ēá --E.M.E. iāé --ié --M.E. ē
(æ:a)--   (ea)   (ə æ:) (ə ɛ :)   (ɛ :)

O.E. Kt. dream(drae/am)--L.O.E. dreám(dream) --
                    E.M.E.   driaé m(dr ə ɛ:m) --
                    M.E.   drem (dr ɛ :m)

Short eo probably smoothed directly to e in Kt., since there is no evidence of any intermediate stage.

eo--e
(eo--e)

O.E. weorc(weork) --M.E.Kt. werk.

medial

ēo--ō
(e:o-e:)

As in the case of the ea diphthong, the variant io, ie, ye spellings suggest a retention of the diphthong in E.M.E., with a shifting of stress and fronting of the second element. The first element then disappeared leaving, in this case, ē.

i.e. O.E. ōo--E.M.E. ēó--ié--M.E. ē
          (e:o)   (eo) (ə e:) (e:)

O.E. Kt. fōond-- E.M.E. fēónd--fiénd-f̄nd
    (fe:ond)   (foond)-(f ə e:nd)-(fe:nd)

io--e

Already in O.E., short io fell in with short eo and developed with it to short e in M.E.

medial
Īo--ō̄

The shifting of stress seems to have affected the development of this diphthong also. With the shifting of stress, the second element fronted to ö, and the diphthong then followed the development of ōo to ē.

O.E. Kt. dīore --E.M.E. dīóre -- diēre -- dōro.

final
ēo, īo--ī
(e:o,i:o--i:)

When these diphthongs appeared finally, there was no shifting of stress, and the development was either through an īe stage to ī, or else directly to ī.

O.E. Kt. frēo/frīo-- E.M. Kt. frīe--frī (or directly
(fre:o,fri:o)   (fri:ə)-(fri:)   to fri)

(24) The development of O.E. diphthongs in M.E. may, then, be summarised as follows:

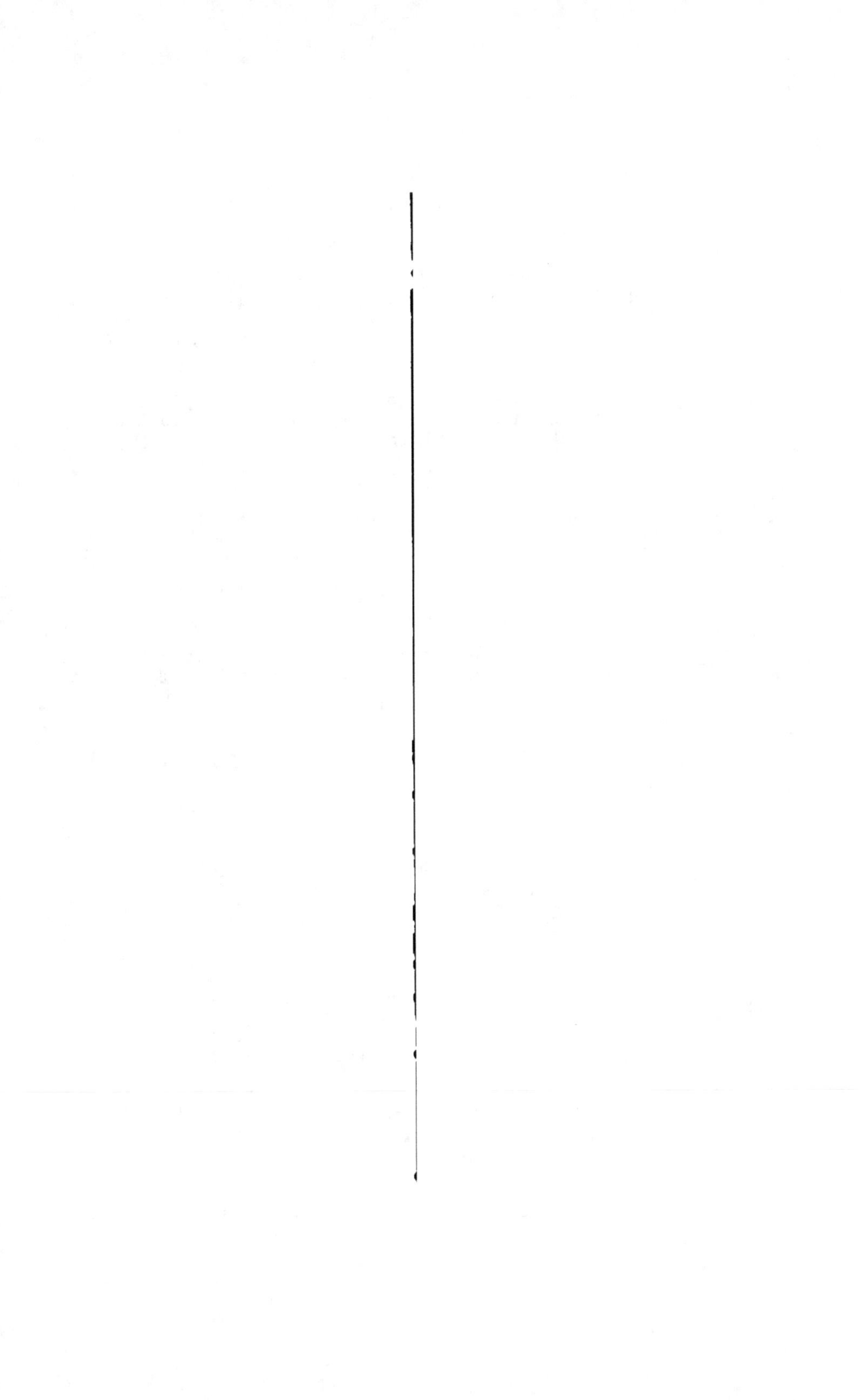

	O.E.	Transition	M.E.
<u>short ea</u> Nth.	ea(æə a)	ae (æ)	a (a)
W.Mid.			a
E.Mid.			a
S.W.			e(ousted by a)
Kt.			a

<u>Conclusion:</u> short ea became short a in M.E. except in S.W., and even here, the S.W. ĕ gave place to ă early in the 14th century.

	O.E.	Transition	M.E.
<u>long ea</u> (Ɛ:ə) Nth.	ēa	ǣea	ⱥ ē
W.Mid.			
E.Mid.			
Kt.	ēa	iaé-ié	ē

<u>Conclusion:</u> O.E. long ea smoothed to long ae everywhere except in Kt., and became long, open e in all dialects in M.E.

	O.E.	Transition	M.E.
<u>short eo</u> Nth.	eo	e (ø) (13th)	e
W.Mid.		e (ø)	e
E.Mid.		(ø)	(ø)
S.W.		(ø)	(ø)
Kt.		e	e

<u>Conclusion:</u> O.E. short eo smoothed to short e in the M.E. period in Nth. and E.Mid. (either directly or through the (ø) stage), and in Kt. In W.Mid. and S.W. it is smoothed to ø and remained.

	O.E.	Transition	M.E.
<u>long eo</u> Nth.	ēo	ē (ø:)	ē
(e;o) W.Mid.		ē (ø:)	ē
E.Mid.		(ø:)	(ø:)
S.W.		(ø:)	(ø:)
Kt.		ié	ē

<u>Conclusion:</u> O.E. long eo became long, close e (e:) in Nth., E.Mid. and Kt. It remained at the (ø:) stage in W.Mid. and S.W.

		O.E.	Transition	N.E.
short io	Nth.	io	i	i

(Short io remained only in Nth. Elsewhere, it became
ēo in O.E.)

long io	Kt.	īo	ió	ō

(Long io remained only in Kt., but in W.S., it fell in
with the development of ēo to ē).

long and short ie.	W.S.	ie	9th i/ie	L.O.E., i/y	M.E. i/y.

It can be seen, then, that O.E. long and short
ŏ became long ǫ and short a respectively; O.E. long and
short eo became N.E. long close e and short e in Nth.,
Mid., and Kt., -- but (ø and ø:) in Mid. and S.E.

47

<u>C H A P T E R   VIII</u>

<u>Phonology: Qualitative Sound Changes: New Diphthongs in M.E.</u>

(25)   The new diphthongs in M.E. were: $\overset{ai}{\wedge}$ei, au, iu, ou, eu.
They arose chiefly in connection with the consonants ȝ, h, and
w; less commonly with f and n, and occasionally with other
consonants.

These consonants developed a glide vowel between themselves and a preceding vowel. This glide fell in with the
original vowel to form a diphthong.

All of the new diphthongs were short. Where a new
diphthong arose from an original long vowel plus a glide, the
diphthong so arising was reduced in quantity from about the
beginning of the 13th century, and fell in with the diphthong
arising from a short vowel plus glide. If a long diphthong was
developed after the 13th century, it was immediately reduced.

(26)   <u>General notes on the new diphthongs.</u>

<u>New diphthongs with h.</u> Before front h -i.e. h preceded
by a front vowel - the glide i was developed. Before back h-i.e.
h preceded b a back vowel - the glide u was developed. The
diphthongs arising as a result were; ei with front h, au and ou
with back h.

48

O.E. eahta -- aehta -- M.E. 3. . ei_hte

O.E. seah -- sach -- M.E. 3. . sau_gh

O.E. boh   -- M.E. bou_gh   *44

(26.1)   The i glide was developed much earlier than the u
glide. *45   In very early M.E. texts, neither appear, but
there are traces of the i glide in 12th century texts, and it
is usual in 13th century texts. On the other hand, the u glide
does not appear until the early 14th century, alt ough there
are a few exceptions to this. (The u glide is found in the
13th century Ancren Riwle). Also, the uniformity of the development of these glides varied with different dialects. It was
far more uniform south of the Humber than north of it. Indeed,
north of the Humber, the u glide was often not ceveloped at all.
(27) New diphthongs with 3 .

before front 3 the glide i was developed, and u resulted
from back 3 . The diphthongs thus formed are: ai and ei with
front 3 ; au and ou with back 3 .   *46

O.E. haegl -- M.E. hail   O.E. 3.mae3den - 3. .. meiden.

O.E. dagns -- M.E. dawes O.E.a3an -- M.E. o3en--o en-o_en
(27.1) The i glide with 3 appeared much earlier than it did
with h. *47   It started in the O.E. period, probably in the
10th century, for in O.E. texts occasional spellings - e.g.
dae ig- indicate its presence. After the development of t e
glide, there as a further development in t at t.e its lf
vocalised to i and was absorbed into the glide. T is, also is
indicated already in O.E. texts where there re occasional

spellings without the g - dael. Therefore, one can say that the
glide and vocalisation of g began in O.E. and was fairly general
in earliest M.E.

Back g in a final position had already become h in O.L.,
so that only medial back g is to be considered here. Medial
back g first labialised to w and then vocalised to u. This
change was much later than that wit front g, since it did not
begin until the 13th century.

Important note. In Kt., the medial back g remained
practically throughout the period, resisting any labialising or
diphthongic tendencies. [*48]

(28)   New Diphthongs with w.

The only glide arising in connection with w was u, and
therefore the diphthongs which developed were au and ou.

O.E. clawu -- M.E. claw / clau   (c.f. sāwol - L.O.E. 5th. sōwel--
                                                     soule
(28.1) Medial and final w appears to have vocalised very early
to u, which then fell in with a preceding vowel to form a
diphthong or a long vowel. That a u glide preceded the vocalisation is fairly definite from the spellings in O.E. texts, here,
even in Beowulf, there are spellings such as hreouw for hr ow.
The occasional forms in L.O.E., from the 10th century on, show
the beginnings of th chan e ich became neral in M. . from
the 12th century on. [*50]

(29)   New diphthongs with other consonants.

Glide vowels ere al o developed in connection ith r,n,

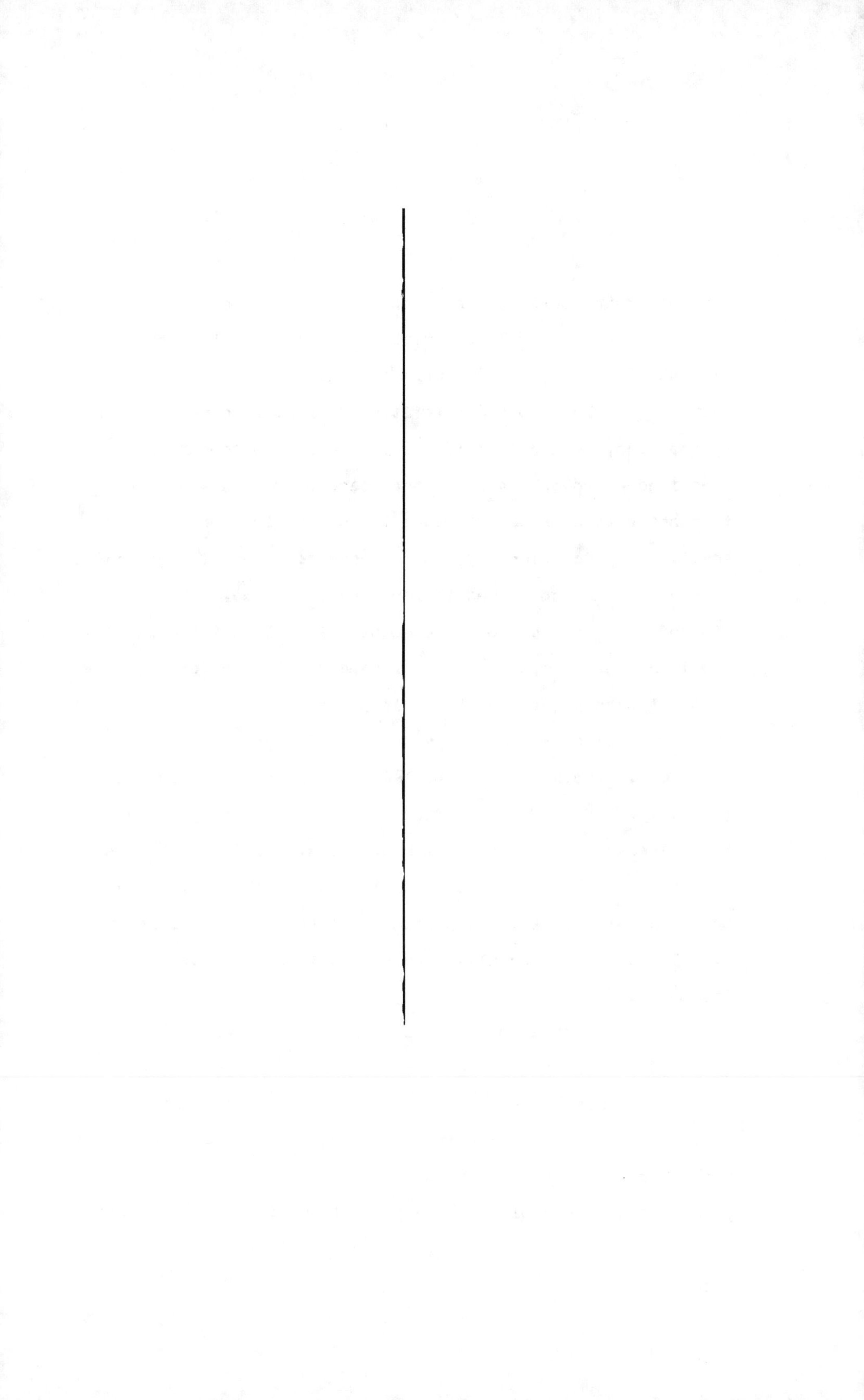

nd the groups sh/nsh. The diphthongs ith f ere etermined by the preceding vowel, but with n only _ei_ resulted, though with sh/nsh both _ei_ and _ai_ were formed.

(29.1) _f._ here voiced f (written v in I.L.) came, throu h syncopation, to stand immediately before a consonant, f vocalised - probably through the stage of r ro u - and fell together with a preceding vowel to form a diphthong or a long vowel. [*] [51] Occasionally, in the same position, f disappeared altogether, and sonetimes it remained unchanged. The vocalising of the consonant occurred most uniformly after a back vowel and before g,k,l. here f came to stand before r,d, or rd the tendency was for it to disappear.

O.L. hafoc -- I.E. hauek -- later hauk

O... hlaefdige -- I.L. lādic (f disappears before d)

(29.2) _n._ Mid.,S. and Kt. have a development peculiar to themselves. In the consonant groups enct, en d, en th, the n develops a glide i between itself and the short preceding e, and then falls together with the vowel to form the diphthong ei. The c or g - the middle consonant then tends to disappear. [*52]

O... drencte (pret. of drencan) -- ... dreinte

O... sengde   "   " sengan   "   seinde

O.. streng f u   "   streinthe

(29.3) _sh/nsh._ Comparatively rarely, but more co only in Mid. than elsewhere, the consonant roups sh/nsh developed glide bet een themselves and a prece in a o e, ic lide

fell in 1th the vowel to form a diphthong.   *53

    O.E. wascan -- M.E. Mid. waishen

      Trensh   Freinsh

(30)   The sources of the new diphthongs may be summarised
        as follows:

ai arose   (1)   in connection with ae plus g
               O.E. daeӡ --10th dae iӡ -- M.E. dai

           (2)   ei, from many sources tended to retract to ai,
               in the second half of the 13th century.
               O.E. weӡ -- 10th wei ӡ -- M.E. wei --13th wai.

           (3)   in connection with sh (sporadically)
               O.E. ae cse --M.F. Mid. aishe

ei arose   (1)   in connection with long ee, long and short eo,
               and front vowels plus h.
               O.E. hēah - L.O.E. hēh -- M.E. heigh
               O.E.rcoht -- M.O.E. rcht --M.E. reight

           (2)   in connection with g preceded by long or
               short e, long ae, and long ea.
all of these   O.E. wregde -- L.O.E. vreigce --M.E. wreide
ei's became ai   O.E. bēag   L.O.E. bēg   M.E. bei
in 13th.   O.E. grāeg   L.O.E. grāeig   M.E. grei

               long eo plus g
               O.E. flēogan --L.O.E. flēgan -- fleien

           (3)   in connection with n plus consonant (occasional)
               O.E. blencte --M.E. bleinte (common in Chaucer)

           (4)   in connection with sh (occasional)
               O.E. flaesc -- M.E. flesh/fl ish

au arose   (1)   in connection with h preceded by long and short
               ae, and long a (with shortening)
               O.E. saeh --M.E. Mid. sah --sauh
               O.E. tāhte --tāhte -- taughte

           (2)   in connection with g preceded by back vowels.
               O.E. dragan --M.E. drauen (often spelled awen)

<u>ou</u> arose   (3)   in connection with w
                            O.E. clawu -- M.E. claue (often spelled
                                             ith w)

                        (4)   in connection with f after back vowels and
                            before g,k,l.
                            O.E. nafogār -- M.E. nauger (anger)

<u>ou</u> arose   (1)   In connection with back vowels plus h
                            O.E. dohtor -- M.E. doughter

                        (2)   in connection with back vowels plus g.
                            O.E. bōga -- M.E. boue

                        (3)   in connection ith back vowels plus w.
                            O.E. cnāwan -- M.E. knōwen --knoue

<u>iu</u> arose   from the vocalisation of w after i
                            O.E. stiward -- M.E. stiuard

<u>eu</u> arose   from the vocalisation of w preceded by
                            O.E. long ea.
                            O.E. fēawe   //M.E. feue

<u>Note</u>. oi was borrowed from the French during the M.E. period,

      but was not a M.E. development.

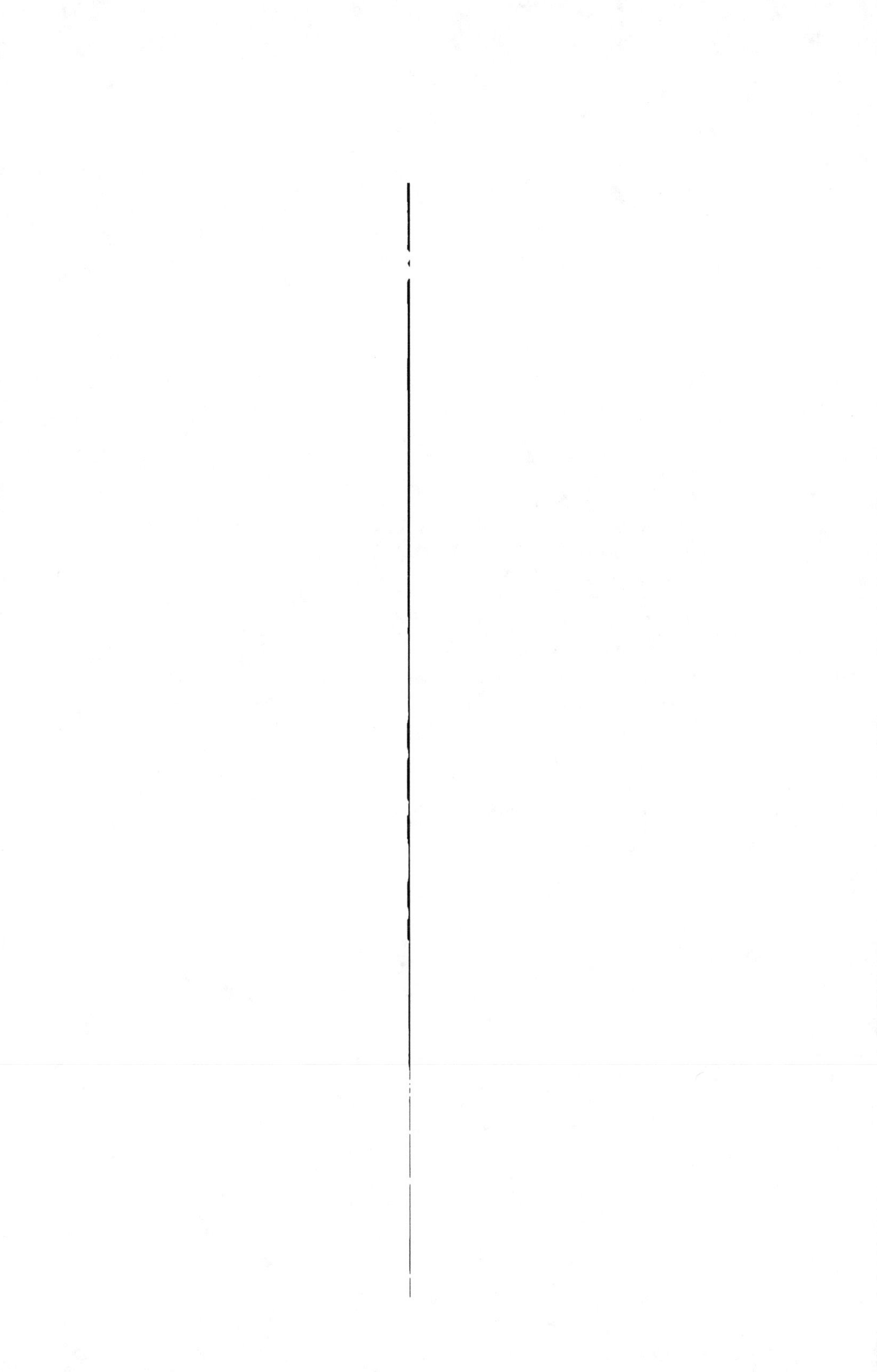

(e) <u>h</u> initially before l, r, m, n, and medially
then alone, h disappeared; elsewhere, it remained except in a few cases when h became f.

(32) <u>Combinative changes.</u>

(32.1) <u>Vocalisation.</u> When the consonants w and ʒ occurred
between vowels or finally after a vowel, they vocalised and
fell in with the preceding vowel or diphthong. [54]

Thus, daeʒ -- dae iʒ -- dai; O.E. sāw(o)l --M.E.3th.soule.
Apart from this vocalisation, there was another one of ʒ
in the prefix ʒe. In this case, the ʒ became i, and the resulting ie smoothed to i/y. Hence O... ʒewiss became M.E. iwiss or
ywiss.

Also, final w after a consonant vocalised to u. O.E. narwe--
M.E. naru. These changes are common to all dialects.

(32.2) <u>Unvoicing.</u> The special M.E. developments concern g and d
finally, and are chiefly found in Nth. and .Mid. [55]

In .Mid. particularly, in final ng, the g unvoiced to k.
O.E. Þing -- .Mid. Þink ; O.E. ʒong -- .Mid. ʒonk.
Chiefly in Nth. and .Mid., d tended to unvoice to t in
final unaccented syllables. This change is most noticeable in
the preterite and past participles.

O.E. lufode --M.E. Nth. lufit

(32.3) <u>Assimilation.</u> This change is noticeable in O.E., but
continues in M.E. The consonants concerned are th dentals
d, t and t,ʒ; ln nd nl; and the labials f and m.

M.E. nd Þat -- nd tat; .L. Þe -- atte; clnc -- clle;
... wifman -- wimmon.

55

(32.4) <u>Disappearance of consonants</u>. Many unstressed consonants disappeared during the M.E. period. The most noticeable are: ch, k, l, n, v (older f), and w. [56]

Final <u>ch</u>, unaccented, disappeared in L.M.E. This accounts for the first person pronoun, <u>I</u>.

O.E. ic -- E.M.E. ich. L.M.E. I.

It also accounts for the suffix <u>ly</u> from E.E. lic.

O.E. wislic -- E.M.E. wislich -- L.M.E. isli/ wisly.

<u>K</u> disappeared intervocalically in the preterite and past participle. O.E. macode -- M.E. makede -- L.M.E. made.

<u>L</u> disappeared before and after ch in Mid. and Sth. dialects.

O.E. mycel -- M.E. Mid. and Sth. muche /miche, beside Nth. mikel.

<u>n</u> disappeared generally in unstressed syllables, but two of the most striking are those of the indefinite article and the possessive pronouns.

O.E. an -- M.E. a h n the next word began with a consonant.

O.E. min -- M.E. mi.

<u>v</u> from older f disappeared before consonants.

O.E. hlaford -- M.E. Sth. lov(e)rd -- L.E. lord.

<u>w</u> disappeared after a consonant and before a back vowel.

O.E. swa -- M.E. Sth. s(w)o -- so.

(32.5) <u>Inserted consonants</u>. In certain positions, consonants were inserted in order to facilitate pronunciation. <u>b</u> as inserted between m-l and m-r: slumbren, Fimble. d as placed between l-r, n-r: alder, pound er. t as place between s-n:listh/ten. [57]

56

(32.6) Metathesis. This phenomen occurred in O.E., but
appears also in M.E., chiefly in the Nth. dialect.

    O.E. brid -- M.E. Nth bird.

(33) Isolative changes. The consonants with which these
changes are most concerned may be grouped as follows: f, ꝑ s;
sc; c; g; and h.

(33.1) f, ꝑ, s. Generally, these three remained, but Kt. and
Sth. in E.M.E f, ꝑ, s, became their voiced equivalents when they
occurred initially. Hence, O.E. for appears here as vor; O.E.
sunne -- zunne; and C.L. ꝑae t -- ðat. *58

    Moreover, in all dialects, became d before and after
liquids: burdene, murdren.

(33.2) sc During the greater part of the O.E. period, the sound
was probably sk. In L.O.E., another pronunciation began to
develop, so that there were two sounds in M.E.

    (a) In all positions except medially before and finally
after a back vowel, the sk sound probably became (s x) which
survived until the 11th century, and then became a pure
sibilant, sh (ʃ).

    O.L. sccal --(s xea 1)-- M.L. shall (ʃal)

    Quite early in the 12th century, this sound was written
sh/sch, which became the normal symbols. In the 14th, French
scribes also wrote it as ss/s, and this mode survived for a
considerable time in Kt. *59

    O.E. scip appears as M.E. ship/schip/ssip/sip.

(b) Medially before and finally after a back vowel, the sk sound was retained and written sk: O.E. dusc -- M.E. dusk. *60

here there was opportunity for levelling-in noun nd verb forms - in nearly all cases the sh is levelled throughout.

O.E. fisc -- sk sound in L.O.E. -- M.E. fish

O.L. fiscas - sk sound in L.O.L.-- M.E. fiskes, but <u>sh</u> is
levelled through.

(33.3) <u>c</u> O.E. c had two values. It was front where it occurred before a front vowel and also finally after i. It was back c elsewhere. These two sounds developed differently in M.E. *61

The regular development of the front c was as follows: at first, in the C.E. period, it probably became a front explosive continuant - (k χ); this survived until the beginning of the 10th century, when the first element became dental - (t χ); then in the 12th century, it assibilated to the tsh (t ʃ) sound, and the symbol ch was adopted from the French. This is the symbol used for it during most of the M.E. period, with cch to indicate geminated c.

Apart from this regular development, there are apparent irregularities. <u>k</u> is frequently found where the front <u>ch</u> is expected.

There are several reasons for this.

(a) The k is sometimes due to the influence of . .
cognates: M. . mikel i probably from . . mil.

(b)   It is sometimes due to the levelling of cognate O.E.

forms in weak veros, in nouns, and in related

dialectal forms:

    O.E. þenc(e)st -- M.E. thinkst, and this k is levelled
    into the infinitive to give thinken where thinch en
    should occur.

    O.E. cīcen should become M.E. chichen, but O.E. cīcenas
    (pl) gives M.E. chiken and this k is levelled
    through.

    W.S. cealf should become M.E. chelf, but unglocalf --
    M.E. Mid.Nth calf and this form survives.

(c)   In unstressed syllables, ch often disappeared:

    O.E. ic -- M.E. I

Back c remained in M.E., and was sometimes still

written c, but where it came to stand before a front vowel

(through umlaut or some other change), it was written k. It

was also written k finally and before n.

    O.E. drincan -- M.E. drinken, O.E. folc --M.E. folk,
                      cniht --knight.

(33.4) ᵹ In O.E., this symbol represented four sounds: (a)
a back [32] explosive in nᵹ and ᵹᵹ (b) a front explosive in nᵹ
and ᵹᵹ ; (c) a back continuant with back vowels; (d) a front
continuant when in connection ith front vowels.

(a) This sound regularly remains and is written g from
the first half of the 12th century: M.E. goᵹe, sinᵹen.

(b) Already in O.E. front nᵹ and ᵹᵹ had assibilated to
the (d z h) sound or dᵹ, but from about the first half of the
12th century, it came to be written j or g .

    O.E. hryoᵹ   -- M.E. Sth. riᵹe (d z h),(d ᵹ)

(c) Already in O.E., initial back ȝ had become explosive g,
and final ȝ had unvoiced to the continuant h sound and as
commonly so written. Therefore, by the M.E. period, only
medial continuant ȝ remained.

O.E. ȝōs -- M.E. ȝōs, O.E. bōȝ -- M.E. bōh.

The medial back continuant normally began to labialise to
w and vocalise to u, possibly as early as the beginning of the
13th century in S. .; somewhat later in Mid. and Wth.; and last
of all in Kt.

O.E. draȝ an -- M.E. drawen.

After a liquid, l/r, which was preceded by a back vowel,
this ȝ labialised <u>but did not vocalise to u.</u> O.E. morȝ en --
M.E. mor e(n).

After a front vowel and before a back vowel, ȝ developed
differently. South of the Humber, very early in M.E., probably
early in the 12th century, back ȝ in this position tended to
become front again, owing to the weakening of the back vowel
to e, hence the ȝ in this position developed as a regular
front ȝ .

O.E. niȝ on -- E.M.E. niȝ en (becomes front and vocal-
ises *nīien -- nīn.

However, north of the Humber in such a position, ȝ remained a back continuant and did not vocalise. On account of
the characteristic an early loss of inflections in t e north,

medial ʒ frequently came to stand finally, in which case it
unvoiced to h and tended to disappear altogether.

O.E. Faʒe -- M.E. .th. āʒe -- āghe (back written -h)
-- ē (Barbour's Bruce)

(d) The front continuant ʒ usually remains initially in M...
and is written until the 14th century, when it begins to be
written y. Where it occurs initially before i/i, it generally
disappeared in .E. early in the 14th century.

O.E. ʒif -- M... ʒif/yif -- L.M.E. if.

Medially and finally, front continuant ʒ developed a
glide, vocalised, and fell in with the glide (see .E. new
diphthongs) to produce a diphthong.

(33.5) h There are three developments of h to consider.
(a) Initially, h remained except where it occurred before
liquids or nasals, where it disappeared completely in .E.;
and in some unstressed words.

O.E. hlnford -- M... -lo(v)rd; o.E. hit has become it
                                    lready in Orme.

(b) Medially, h only remained when it was geminated or when
it was with another consonant, and here it was a front or back
continuant. In the group ht it came to be written in many
ways: ʒt, ʒht, -ht, cht (Lith.), and gt occasionally.

Finally, h generally remains a voiceless continuant,
written -h etc. However, in some districts in the west, even
final h tends to become labial f at the beginning of the 14th
century. In some instances, f is actually written for
final h. *C3

61

O.E. þurh -- E.E. thur h, but is sometimes written thurf in the 14th.

(c)   hw develops differently in the south and in the north In the south the labial element becomes more important than the h, and so the sound is written wh, or, in some dialects, simply w.

E.E. hwæt -- E.E. 3th. what/w at.

In the north, the h becomes an explosive k, and hw becomes kw.   This sound is represented in several ways - cu, cw, cuh, cwh.   *64

Nth. cua, qwu, cuha, cwha

O.E. hwā --

3th. who, wo

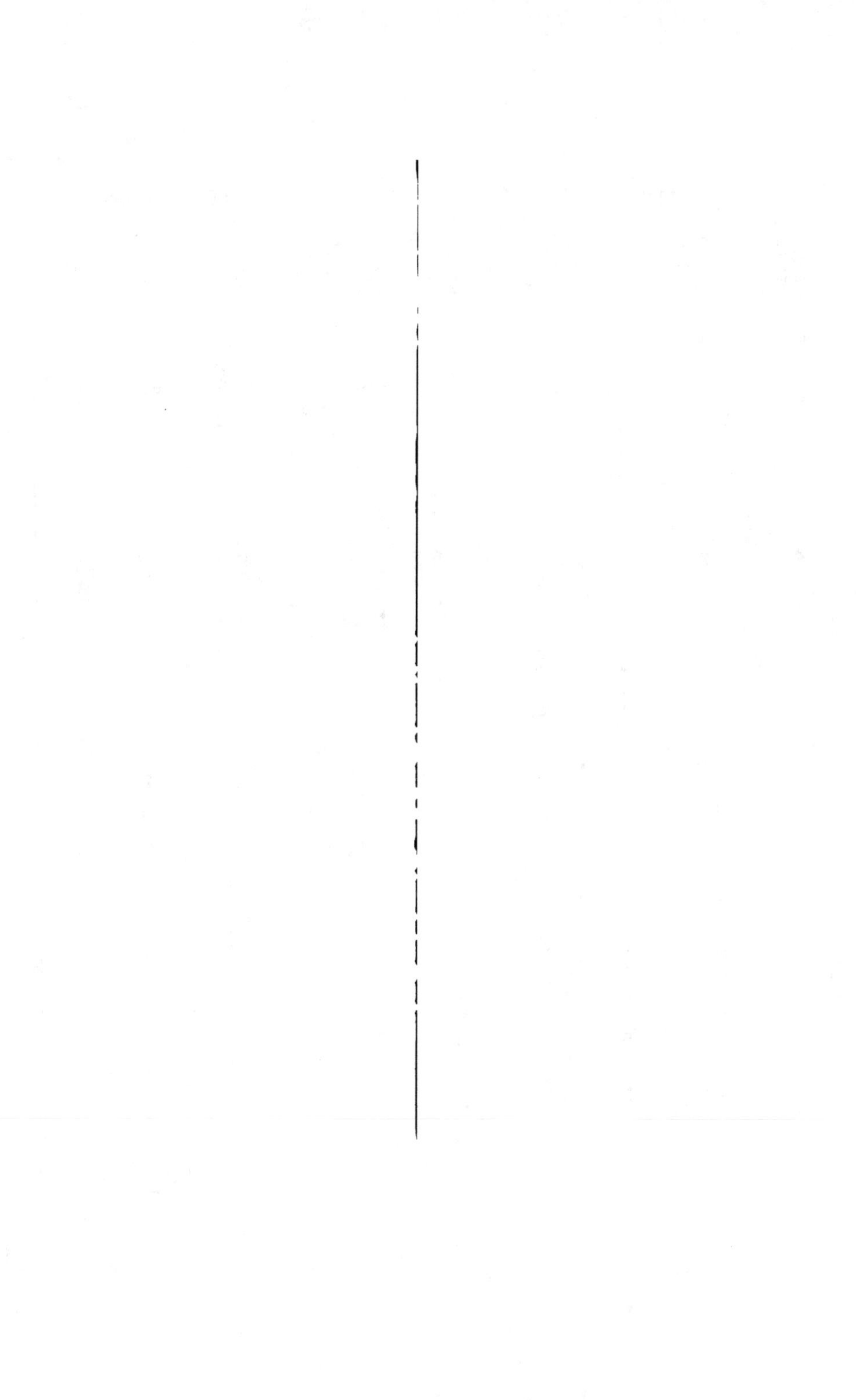

THE DEVELOPMENT OF ... OF LI ... I...

	10th	11th	12th	13th	14th

c

Ft. al.   k x   t x   t ʃ (wr.ch)   in unstressed syl

k. ral.   k   k   k ʃ   disappears finally

   disappears bet. vowels in pret and ust articiple

f

voiced   f   Assimilates to m in groups fn, fm in O.E. and M.E. periods.

(disapped s plus cons.) f , written v

(palatals)

Bk.Pal. Expl.   n ʒ ,ʒʒ   n ʒ,ʒʒ   wr.n ,ss   ng,   n ,

t.Pal "   n ʒ ;ʒʒ   d ʒh,dʒ   wr.ss/s

t.Pal.Cont.

Initially   ʒ   ʒ   ʒ   ʒ

Medial, Final   ʒ   i ʒ --ii   i   i   r.y   i

Bk.Pal.Cont.

Initial   ʒ   expl.   remained

Final   ʒ   cont.h

Medial   ʒ   ʒ   ʒ   (early, O.E.)Mid L t Kt.

--w--u   --w--u   --w--u

h

Initial   h   lost before l,m,n,r; in unstressed words

Medial ht   ht   ht   ht ritten t,ʒ ht,ʒcht,cht(Nth.),ct

Medial hh   hh   hh   hh--f? (written uh)

n

Assimilates to l in ln group, to me in mn group-both O.E. and M.E.

ʒ

sc

Medial,Final

after bk.vowel   sk   sk   sk   sk   sk

Other,sk--   s x   sh   sh (written sh,sch;ss,s in Kt.)

w

Medial, Final

with vowels   w   w   w ---u   u   u

(after a consonant, before a bk,vowel w disappears)

63

SUMMARY OF THE CHIEF DIALECTAL DIFFERENCES IN THE CONSONANTS.

	Nth.	W.Mid.	S.Mid.	S.W.	n.t.
<u>d</u>	d(t unaccented)	d	d(t unaccented)	d	d
<u>f</u>	f	f	f	f(v initially)	f(v initi lly)
<u>Bk.Pal.nʒ</u> }ᶜ	nɡ }e	nɡ }ᵉ	nɡ/nk }ᵉ	nɡ i	nɡ i
<u>h</u> Final / hw	h / k	h / wh	f? / wh	f? / .h	h / ιh
<u>l</u>	l	lost plus ch in other dialects			
<u>r</u>	metachesis	otherwise remains			
<u>s</u>	ʒ	s	s	s(z initially)	s(z initially)
<u>þ</u>(voiceless) þ	þ	þ	þ	þᵗð ")	þᵗð ")

64

CHAPTER X

Accidence; Introduction.

(35)   There was a general weakening, in M.E., of the vowels
a, o, u, in unstressed positions. They tended to become the
indeterminate vowel sound (ə), which was usually written e.
However, it was frequently written u in Mid. and i in Nth[*65]
Moreover, unstressed syllables tended to weaken and disappear.
This is particularly noticeable in inflectional endings with
final m or n.

As a rule, the weakening and disappearance of unstressed
vowels and syllables took place much earlier in the north than
elsewhere. The Mid. development was usually about a century
behind that of the Nth., and the Southern was later still.[*66]
This difference was probably owing to the fact that the north
was extensively settled by Danes, who spoke a language closely
related to English, and hence they found the root words more
important than the unfamiliar inflectional endings, which they
disregarded.

(35.1)   Weakening occurred, to a greater or less degree, in the
following positions: inflectional endings, suffixes and prefixes, medial syllables, and unaccented words.

The inflectional ending - um, of the ... dative plural,
became - un, which became - en (ən), and then the n tended to
disappear. O.E. dagum--dagun--da en--a e(n).

The vowels of unstressed suffixes became (ə).

The weakening in <u>prefixes</u> was slightly different. It occurred only in the prefixes of verbs, and chiefly in those containing a long vowel, which shortened. Also, the prefixes of -, on -, ond-, all became -a-.
O.E. ārisen M.E. ărisen; O.E. ondlong M.E. along.

In medial syllables, the vowel frequently weakened to such an extent that it disappeared altogether.
O.E. hēafod--M.E. hēv(e)d --hēd.

Early in M.E., the e in <u>unstressed words</u> disappeared.
O.E. sif nes -- M.E. sinnes -- sin(e)s -- sins.

(36)   <u>The effect of weakening on the inflectional system.</u>
It must be remembered that all of the changes in the inflectional endings were much earlier and more radical in the Nth. and Mid. dialects than in the southern ones.
(36.1) <u>Nouns.</u> All but a very few nouns had gone over to the old 'a' declension by the end of the M.E. period. By this time, there were only two endings; e and es. The third ending, en, of the 'a' declension dative plural had been ousted. The -es ending expressed the genitive singular and all the plural cases; and -e, when it occurred, stood for the other singular cases.

66

(36.2) __Adjectives and the article.__ The inflectional endings
of the adjectives and the article almost entirely disappeared
during the M.E. period. In the Nth. and Mid., they had disappeared entirely before the 14th century, but in the south,
inflectional e of the adjective was retained, though the indeclinable article, __the__, was generally used. Indeed, in the
North and E.Mid., these inflections had practically disappeared
by 1200.

An important result of the loss of inflections in the
adjective and the article was the consequent loss of grammatical
gender in English.

(36.3) __Pronouns.__ The weakening of inflections in pronouns had
resulted in such confusion that it led to the adoption of new
forms in Nth. and E.Mid. These forms were subsequently generalised in N.E. From about 1300 on, in Nth. and L.Mid., the
pronominal forms scho/sche, they, their, them appear. They
were borrowed from Scandinavian forms. At this period, .Mid.
and the southern dialects still cling to the native forms,
ho, hy, etc.

(36.4) __Verbs.__ There are three outstanding changes in verbal
inflections. (a) In Mid.and Nth. by the 14th century the -s
ending of the present indicative third singular and all plural
forms has taken the place of O... th. However, th was
preserved in the south.
(b) The infinitive had lost ll ending in Nth. by the 14th
century, while in the southern dialects -en and -e are kept.

(c) O.E. -ende of the present participle became -and$ in Nth.;
inde in E. . and Kt.; ande/ende in Mid., although this gave
place to later inge, which survived in N.E..

(37)   <u>Dialectal differences in inflections.</u> [67]

 <u>Northern</u> is distinguished by the early loss of endings
in nouns, adjectives and the article; by the pronominal form
scho, and the early adoption of they/ their/them; by the -s
ending of the present indicative; by the loss of the infinitive
ending; and by the participial and.

 <u>E.Mid.</u> resembles Nth. except - in the pronominal sche;
in the e/en infinitive ending, and in the ende/ande ending of
the present participle with its change to inge.

 <u>W.Mid.</u> clings to traditional forms much longer than
either Nth. or E.Mid., though it does accept the present
indicative -s, and has the characteristic Mid.-inge development
in the participle.

 <u>S.W. and Kt.</u> retain the traditional forms almost entirely
until the end of the period, although the weakening of endings
in the nouns led to some confusion.

68

CHAPTER XI

Accidence; Nouns and Adjectives.

(39)   Nouns. At the end of the M.E. period, the nouns, with
a few exceptions, had all gone over to the masculine a- declension. That is, their inflectional endings were: (e),es (e),
in the singular; and -es throughout the plural. These endings
in the a- declension in L.E. were the result, partly of weakening
in inflections, and partly of analogical levelling. *68
That is,

```
O.E. N.A. fisc      should have become M.E. fish    and appears as fisl
      G    fisces     "      "      "      '    fishes  "      "    as fishe:
      D    fisce      "      "      "      "    fish(e) "      "    " fish
Plural
      N.A. fiscas     "      "      "      "    fishes  "      "    " fishes
      G    fisca      "      "      "      "    fish(e) "      "    " fishes
      D    fiscum     "      "      "      '    fishe(n) "     "    " fishes
```

In the genitive and dative plural, the -es of the nominative has
been levelled through so that there is only one plural form,
fishes.

(39.1) The a- declension neuters differed from the masculines
only in the formation of the ... plural, and therefore they
were early included in the general declension.

```
O.E. N.A. sing. word gives ... ord; M.E. plu. ord should give ord
                but the masculine N.A. is levelled throu  into orde.
```

69

O.E. N.A. sing. <u>scip</u> gives M.E. <u>ship</u>; plural <u>scipu</u> should give
M.E. <u>shipe</u>, but <u>shipes</u> appears by analogy with the
masculine forms.

(39.2)   The genitive and dative plural of all of the O.E.
declensions (except genitive in the weak declension) had the
same endings. Consequently, it is not surprising that, when
-es was adopted for these endings in the a- declension, the
one ending became common to all declensions. From that point,
it was natural to make all plurals uniform by adopting -es in
the N.A. also.

O.E. plur.(fem)

N.A.	glōfa	should give M.E.	clōve,	but appears as	glōves
G.	glōfa	' " "	clōve	" "	" glōves
D.	glōfum	" " "	glōve(n)"	"	" clōves

(39.3)   In the singular, nouns whose oblique cases ended in
a vowel differed only in the genitive from the a-declension
nouns ending in -e.

O.E. Masc. -a	M.E.	O.E. Masc, -u	M.E.	
N.	ende	ende	sunu	sune	
A. ende	ende	sunu	sune	
G. endes	<u>endes</u>	suna	<u>sune</u>	sunes is adopt-
D.	ende	ende	suna	sune	ed from the a-declension.

This levelling process was carried through all declensions
until there were only a few exceptions to the uniform declension
at the end of the M.E. period.

(39.4)   <u>The result of this levelling was that grammatical
gender disappeared.</u>

70

(40)   <u>Dialectal differences in inflections durin the .E. period</u>

All of the chanes connected with accidence took place much earlier in the north than in the south, and the uniform declension became general in the north lon before it did in the south.

(40.1) Nouns which had ended in a vowel in O.L. retained an indeterminate vowel ending until the end of }.E. in some dialects, but lost it early in others.

O.E. ende -- ".E. Jth. end   O.E. sunu --I.... Nth. son
              Sth. ende   Jth. sone

(40.2) In the "th. dialect, the obscure vowel of the ".E. endins was frequently written <u>i</u>: tratour<u>is</u> (see Barbour's Bruce) while in ".Mid. this vowel was often written <u>u</u>: ship<u>us</u>.

(40.3) While all nouns tended early to go over to the a- declension in the Jth. and Mid. dialects, the tenency in J. . and At. for some time during the ".E. period was towards the weak declension. [*69] The obscure vowel of the weak nominative singular was felt, in those dialects, to be an indication of singular number, while the -en ending of the nominative plural was looked upon as an indication of a plural number. Hence, -e was levelled throughout the singular, and all nouns ending in -e ere given a plural in -en. Many other nouns, not endin in -e were also inflected in this way.

(40.4) The declension of the O. . words <u>fisc</u> and <u>nana</u> mi ht, therefore, appear in the first half of the 14th century as follows:

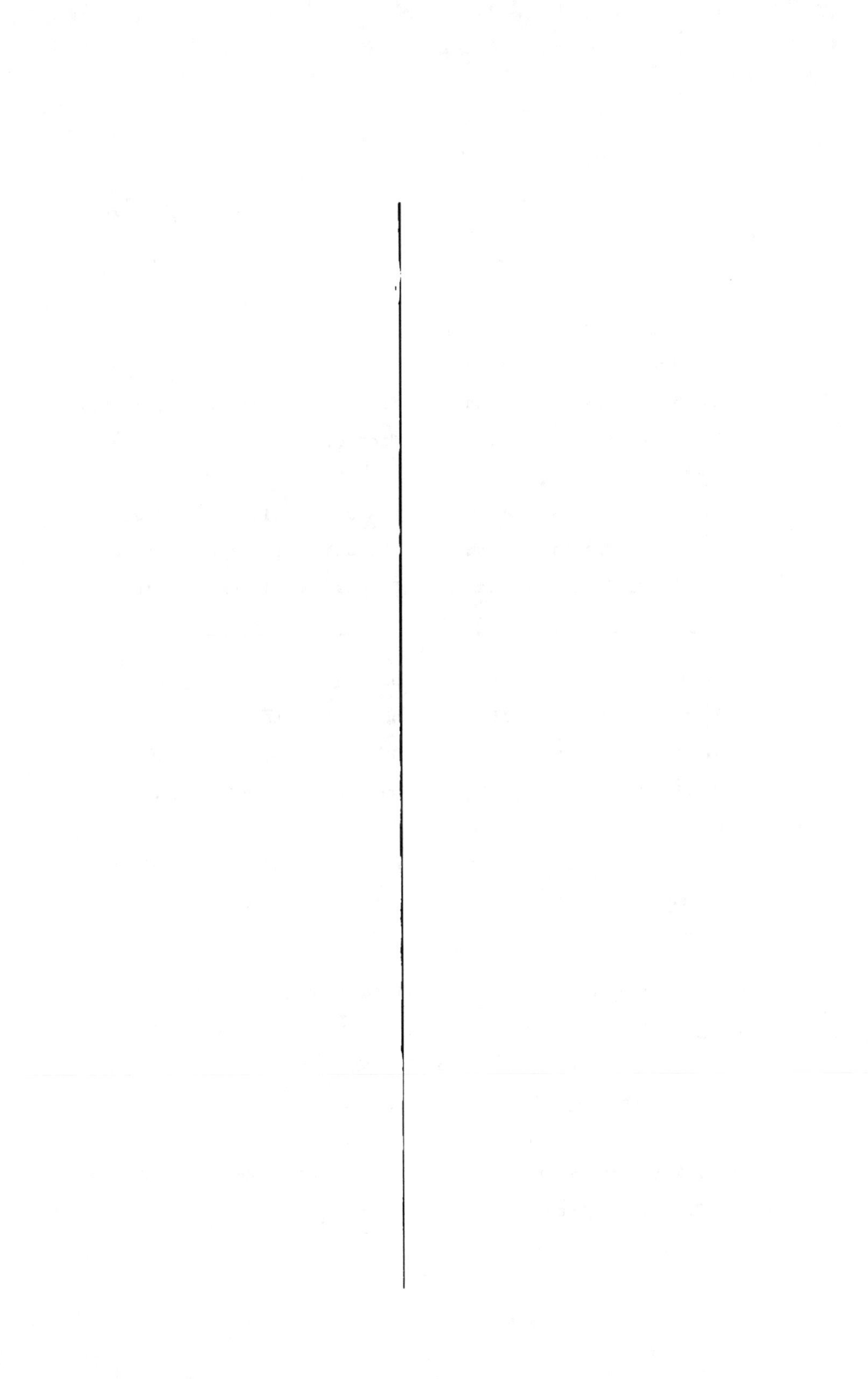

	O.E.	Nth.	E.Mid.	W.Mid.	S.	Kt.
N.A.	fisc	fish	fish	fish	fishe	fische
G.	fisces	fishis	fishes	fishus	fishe(s)	fishe(s)
D.	fisce	fish	fish	fish(e)	fishe	fishe

Plural

N.A.	fiscas	fishis	fishes	fishus	fishen	fishen
G.	fisca	fishis	fishes	fishus	fishe/ene	fishe/ene
D.	fiscum	fishis	fishes	fishus	fishen	fishen

N.	nama	nām	nāme	nōme	nāme	nāme
A.	naman	nām	nāme	nōme	nāme	nāme
G.	naman	nāmis	nāmes	nōmus	nāme	nāme
D.	naman	nām	nām	nōm(e)	name	nāme

Plural

N.A.	naman	nāmis	nāmes	nōmus	nāmen	nāmen
G.	namena	"	"	"	nāme/ene	nāme/ene
D.	namum	"	"	"	nāmen	nāmen

(41)   <u>Exceptions</u>. There is a limited number of nouns whose
<u>plurals</u> differ from those of the uniform declension.

(a)   Three of these nouns probably show the effect of the S.
and Kt. levelling of -en in the plural.

The plurals are: oxen, children, and brethren.

<u>oxen</u>. This form is the only true eak plural that survives to-day.

    O.E. oxa gives ... ox(e) which gives N. . ox
         oxan ' " oxen '   "   "   oxen

<u>children</u>. The form is an instance of a double plural. The O.E. nominative plural ended in -ru. This ending has been kept, but the weak -en ending has been added to it.

    O.E. cild gives M.E. child and M.E. child
         cildru   "   " childre "   "   childer, which does
         survive in some dialects, but usually -en has been added
         to the vowel ending.

<u>brethren</u>. This form is another instance of the double plural, where the -n was added according to the S.E. and Kt. tendency. However, in this case, the umlauted vowel of the dative singular has been levelled into the plural, by analogy with the plurals of the monosyllabic declension; mann, menn, etc. That is, there are really three plural forms in this one word: the -r plural of the original declension, the -en plural of the weak declension, and the umlauted plural of the monosyllabic declension.

    O.E. N. sing. brōðor   M.E. brother
          D. "   brēðor   brether (disappeared)
          N. plur. brōðor/ru   brother(s added analogically)
                                         or brethren.

(b)   The other nouns which withstood the movement for uniformity belonged to one declension - the monosyllabic. Here, the plurals, which differed from the singulars in the root vowel, survived into M.E.
Among these nouns are: goose, geese; man, men; tooth, teeth; foot, feet; and so forth.

     It is to be noted that, in all of these nouns with the irregular plurals, the -es of the genitive plural is regularly added to the other plural ending or endings.

73

(42)   <u>Adjectives.</u> By the end of the ..L. period, the only
adjectival ending left was -e, and all distinction of gender
had disappeared. In Nth. amd .id., even the -e had gohe, and
the adjectives were entirely uninflected. [70]

In 3. . and .t., the -e remained to mark the weak
declension, used when the adjective was preceded by an article,
a possessive or a demonstrative; adjectives of the strong
declension when they ended in a vowel in C.L., and all plurals.
(42.1) In earlier ".L. texts, there were many traces of the
fuller adjectival inflections, and even as late as 1340, in the
.entish 'Agenbite of Inwit', the weak -en ending can be found.
<u>.eak declension:</u>

Generally by the middle of the period, the inflectional
vo.els had all weakened to -e, and the final -n's had disappeared. [71]

<u>Singular.</u>	I.E.	
Masc.		
N. swifta	swifte	
A. swiftan	swifte(n)	
G. swiftan	swifte(n)	All of these forms,
D. swiftan	swifte(n)	
		and all those of
<u>Plural</u>		the other genders
N.A. swiftan	s'ifte(n)	
C. swiftan/ena	swifte(n/ene became <u>swifte</u> in L.
D. swiftan	swifte(n)	

(42.3)   <u>Strong declension ending in a vowel.</u>[72] This declension
seems to have become confused with the weak declension whose
nominatives also ended in a vowel, and so by the end of the ...
period (in the south), the declension .ad one form its final -e

<u>Singular.</u>   M.E.

Masc. N. clēne   clene
       A. clēnne   clenne
       G. clēnes   clenes
       D. clēnum   clene(n)

Fem.   N. clēnu   clene   In L.M.E.,<u>clene</u> was the
       A. clēne   clene
       G. clēnre   clenre/er   form throu·hout this
       D. clēnre   clenre/er
                                        declension.

Neut. N. clēne   clene
       A. clēne   clene
       G. clēnes   clenes
       D. clēnum   clene(n)

<u>Plural</u> (all genders)

    N. A. clēne   clene
       G. clēnra   clenre/er
       D. clēnum   clene(n)

(42.4)   <u>Strong Declension not ending in a vowel.</u>[72]

        The forms for this declension were the same as those
in (42.3) except for the fact that the nominatives of all
genders, and the accusative neuter had no ending.

        All endings had disappeared in the singular in M.E.,
even in the south. In the plural, the -e of the M.E. plural was
levelled throughout the other cases.

			M.E.	L.M.E.
<u>Plural</u>	N.A.	swifte	swifte	swifte
		swiftra	swiftre/er	swifte
		swiftum	swifte(n)	swifte.

CHAPTER III

Pronouns.

(43)   <u>Demonstrative pronouns and the article.</u> The
extensive simplification to be seen in the nouns and adjectives
is evident in the inflection of these pronouns also.

(43.1) <u>The Article.</u> By the end of the ... period, only the
one, indeclinable form t.e þe survived. This one form was
general in Nth. before the end of the 13th century, but in the
south, traces of the inflections can be found even in 14th
century texts.

All ... forms of the article are based on the ...
demonstrative, sē, sēo, þact, o. asc. and en. no. ere
formed in early M.E. — þē and þēo—on the analogy of the other
forms which began ith þ. It is from these forms that the
L.M... þo/the is derived. [*73]

(43.2) <u>The Demonstratives.</u> The ... demonstrative, <u>that, those</u>
is also based on the O.. sē, sēo, þact. In this case, t e
form þat, nich is levelled throughout the singular, comes
from the O.E. neuter nom. The plural form, þō is levelled
from O.E. N.E. plural þā [*74]

The N.E. <u>this, these</u> demonstrative comes on on th ...
þes, þeos, þis. In L.M.E. the t o forms, þes n þis a
used for all cases of the singular ile th our forms, þ is,
þes, þise, þese — re s d in iscriminately in ll case
of the plural.

1. se
2. þone, þæne þon(e), þen(e
3. þæs þes, þas
4. þæm, þan þan, þen, þan.

1. þæt þet, þæt
2. þa þo, þa
3. þæra þer(e), þer(e)

þæt þet, þat
þæs þes, þas
þæn, þan þan, þan, þen

... the masc... þe was lev...
... orms for the article.

...out... þat, that was levelled t...
... or the demonstrative.

þa þo, þa
þæra þer(e), þer(
þæn, þan þa, þan, þo

þæs þes
þisne þisne
þis(s)es þis(s)es, þ
þis(s)um þis(s)en, þ

þeos þeos, þea

<u>Plural</u>   O.E.   M.E.

    N.A. þās   þas, þos
      G. þissa, þissera   þisse, þissere
      D. þissum   þis(s)en, þes(s)e(n).

    þes, þes, þese, þise were the forms used throughout the
    plural for all cases and genders.

(45)   <u>The personal pronouns</u>. The personal pronouns do not
show the same simplification as do the demonstrative pronouns.
Moreover, in the third person pronoun there is considerable
dialectal variation throughout the period, and even at the end
of the period, there is not the same uniformity as there is
in the nouns and pronouns.

(45.1)   <u>The first and second persons</u>. There is little chan_e
from O.E. to M.E. in these pronouns.

        The only changes in the first person were: ich became
I, [75] when the unstressed ch disappeared; us became us in
unstressed positions; [76] and the dual person disappeared at
the end of the period, although it occurs in early texts.
        O.E.   M.E.   <u>Dual</u> O.E.   M.E.
N. ic   ich --I   N. wit   witt
A. me   me   A. uncit/unc   unnc
G. min   mi(n)   G. uncer   unnkerr
D. me   me   D. unc   unnc

(These M.E. dual forms are taken from the dedication to the Ormulum)

<u>Plural</u>
N. we   we
A. ūs   us
G. ūre   ure
D. ūs   us

        The only remarkable change in the second person is the
introduction of the ȝur, ȝou, ȝuw, ȝou forms, [77] from which

the modern second person plural forms are derived. The dual
second person disappears early.

Singular	O.E.	M.E.		O.E.	M.E.
N. þū	þu	Sing.	N.ġē	ȝe	
A. þē	þe	D.A. ēow	ȝow,cu,ow, ȝu, ȝou, ȝow, you	
G. þīn	þi(n)			
D. þē	þe	G. ēower	eower, euer, ower, ȝur, ȝower, your	

(45.3)   <u>The third person</u>. There is considerable dialectal
difference here owing to the adoption in Nth. and E.Md. of new
forms. These forms: she, they, their, them, were not adopted
generally in the south until the 15th century. Therefore, in
the 14th century, M.E. developments from O. . forms were retained in Kt., S.W., and parts of .Mid. *78

Singular	O.E.	Nth.	E.Mid.	Mid	S.W.	Kt.
Masc. N.	hē	he	he	he	he/ha	he/ha
A.	hine	him	him	him	hin(e)	hin(e)
G.	his	his	his	his	his	his
D.	him	him	him	him	him	him
Fem. N.	hīo,hēo hie	scho	scheß o	schc/she he,hue,ho	heo,he,ho hue,hi	heo,he,ho hue,hi
A.	hīo,hēo hie	hire,hir here,her	hire,hir here,her	hire,hir here,her	hire,hir here,her	hie,hire,here
G.	hire	hire,here	hire,here	hire,here	hire,here	hire,here
D.	"	'	"	"	"	'	"	"	'	"
Neut. N.A.	hit	hit	hit,it	hit,it	hit,it	hit,it
G.	his	his	his	hi	his	his
D.	him	him,hit	him,it	him,hit	im,it	him,it

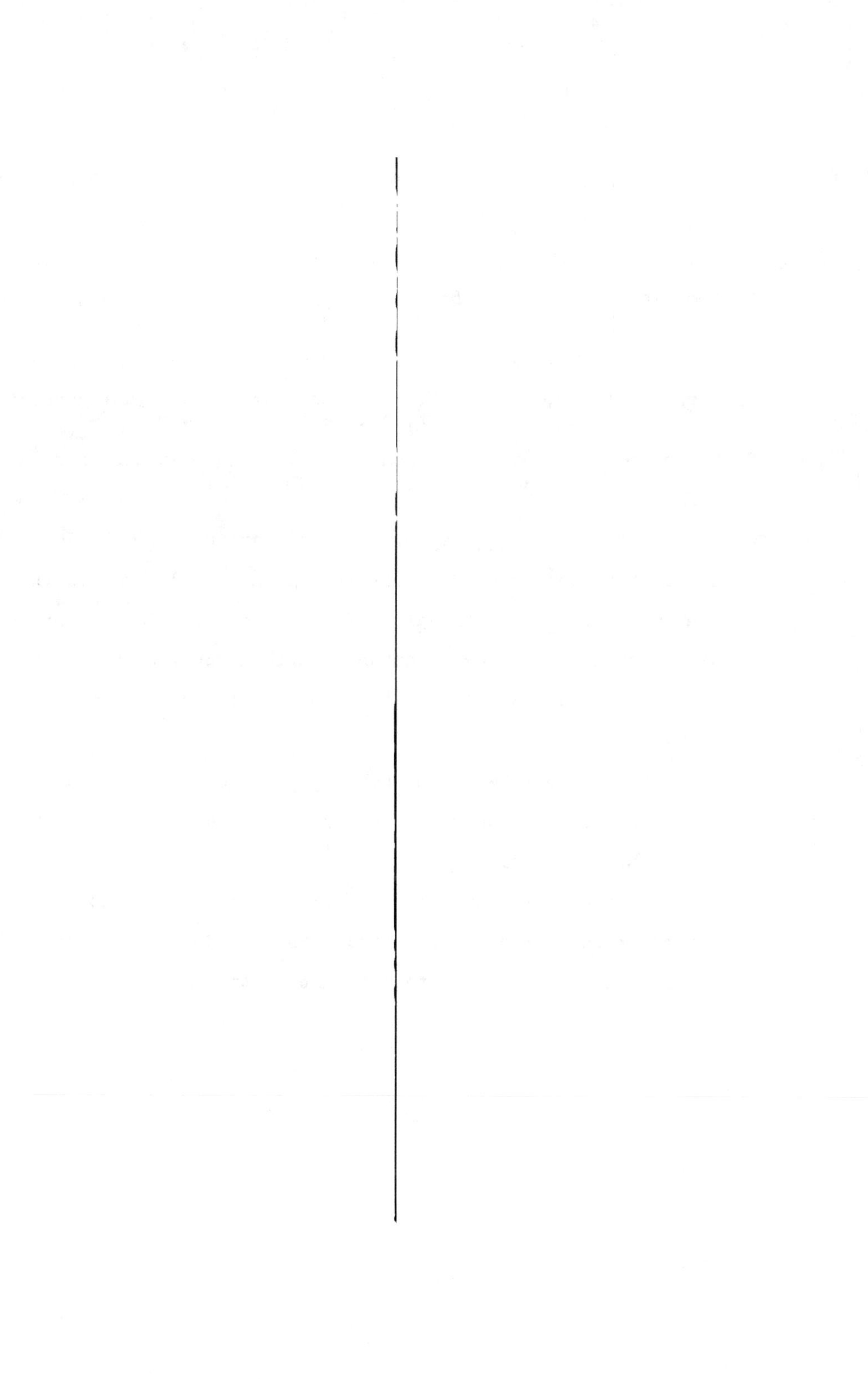

Plural	O.E.	Nth.	L.Mid.	W.Mid.	S.W.	Kt.
N.	heo,hie	thai,they þei,þai	þei,þai he,hi	þai,þei neo	hii,ai,heo	hi,hy
A.	heo,hie	thaym,þeym	hem	hem,hom	ham,hom	ham,hys,his
C.	hira	thair,þair þaire	hyr,here þeyr,ther	nor,hur here	hure,hor here	hare,hire here
D.	him,heom	thaym,þeym	hem,þem	hem,hom heom	hem,ham hom	hem,ham

The forms <u>she,sche,scho</u>, which appear in Nth. and Mid. in the 14th century are of uncertain origin. Wyld suggests that they may represent a blending of O.E. sēo, the fem. demonstrative, and hēo, the fem. pronoun. Certain forms which appear in the 15th century would seem to support this suggestion: sœ, gœ, ȝho, ghe.

On the other hand, the forms <u>they, their, them,</u> and their variants are definitely derived from the Scandinavian plural pronouns, þeir, þeira, þeim.

The greatest change in the personal pronouns, then, occurs in the forms of the third person, and are much more general in Nth. and Mid. than in the southern dialects.

80

CHAPTER XIII:

Accidence; Verbs.

(46)   In O.E. there were two types of verbs: the strong verb,
whose preterite was formed by a change in the stem vowel; and
the weak verb, whose preterite was formed by the addition of a
dental suffix.   These types survive in "...., although there is a
noticeable tendency for strong verbs to go over to the weak class.

Most of the other general changes occurred as a result of
confustion in the preterites.   In the strong verbs, the vowels
of the singular preterite, the plural preterite, and the past
participle were often interchanged, and many new forms arose
through analogy.   Owing to the weakening of vowels, the preterite
vowels of the first two classes of weak verbs became identical
and so these two conjugations fell together in ..E.

There were also certain dialectal differences in the conjugations similar to the differences present in nouns.   That is,
in Nth, the infinitive ending disappeared earlier than else here,
and the obscure vowel was frequently written i; in . id., the
obscure vowel was often written u; and in the southern dialects
the O.E. forms remained longer than in other dialects.

(47)   The strong verbs.   There were seven classes of strong
verbs in O.E.   These were distinguished by the series of vowels
which occurred in the present, preterite singular, preterite
plural and past participle.   The seven vowel series and their

M.E. equivalents are as follows: [79]

I.   ī   ā   i   i   :M.E. ī   ō(ə:)   ā   i   i
      drīfan, drāf, drifon, drifen   driven, drōf(Nth.drāf),driven,driven

II.   ēo   ēa   u   o   ō(e:)   ō(ε:)   ō(ə:)   ō(ə:
      clēofan,clēaf,clufon, clofen   elēfen, clēf   clōven,cloven

II.   i/e   a/ea   u   u/o   i/e   o/a   u   u/o
      bindan, band, bundon, bunden   binden, band(. ' id/bond)bunden,bunden
      meltan, mealt,multon, molten   mälten, malt   multen, molter

IV.   e   ae   ǣ/ē   o   o   a   (ε:)e/e(e:) ō
      beran, bær, bǣron/ē boren   boren, bar,   bĕren/bōren,
                                                                     boren.

V.   e   ae   ǣ/ē   o   e   a   (ε:)/e(e·) e
      tredan, træd, trǣdon/ē,treden   treden, trad,   trōden,trōden,
                                                                     treden

VI.   a   ō   ō   a   a/ae   ā   ō(o:)   o(α) ̄
      faran, fōr, fōron, faren,faeren   fāren, fōr,   fōren,fāren

II.   ǣ/ā   ē   ē   ā/aē   (ε:)/o(ə:) e(e:) e(e:) (ε:)/ō(ə:)
      lǣtan,lēt, lēton,   laeten   lēten, lēt, lētten, lētten

VIII) ea/a   ēo   ēo   ea/a   (ε:)e/o(ə:) e(e:) e(e:) (ε:)/o(ə:)
  WS healdan,hēold,heoldon , healden   hēlden, hēld,hēlden, hēlden
Merc haldan, hēold, "   halden   hōlden   "   "   hōlden

N... The distinctions between the two types of that class
     disappear.

(47.1)   From this survey, it will be seen that there are few changes in those verbs which remained strong that are not in accordance with the regular phonetic changes in M.E. Normally, there are no irregularities in the first and third classes. In the second, fourth, fifth and sixth, the vowels are lengthened where they are short, except in the preterite singular. This follows the normal action of lengthening of vowels in open, accented syllables.

In the second class, the vowel of the past participle is levelled into the preterite plural and a lengthened into the

fourth, fifth and sixth classes, the vowel of the preterite
plural remained, but the vowel of the infinitive in each
class was lengthened, in addition to the vowel of the past
participle.

(47.2) Many analogical forms can be found in M.E. texts beside
the normal ones. Strong verbs frequently developed variant
preterites by analogy with weak verbs: the preterite and past
participle of M.L. <u>cleven</u> had variant forms <u>clēvede, clēved</u> -
or, with shortening - <u>clefte,cleft</u>. New forms arose through
the cross levelling of the vowels of the preterite singular
and plural: the levelling of the singular vowel into the
plural is characteristic of Nth. - O.E. pret.plur. <u>ðruncon</u>
appears in M.E. Nth. as <u>dranc</u>, by analogy with sing.- <u>dranc</u>;
levelling of the plural into the singular was more frequent in
Mid. and Sth. dialects, - O.E. sing. <u>hal</u> appears in M.E. as
<u>hēle</u>, with the vowel from the plural <u>hēlen</u>. Often, the vowel
of the past participle was levelled through both preterites:
the M.E. preterite <u>flōw</u>, beside normal <u>flēw</u> shows the influence of the P.P. <u>flōwen</u>. This particular irregularity is
frequent in the west, to the extent that it is called the
Weston preterite. [80]

83

(48)   The three O.E. classes of weak verbs with their corres-
ponding M.E. forms are as follows: *81

	Inf.	Pret.	P.P.	M.E. Inf.	Pret.	P.P.
I.	an	ede/de/te	ed/d/t	en	ede/de/te	ed/d/t
	deman	demde	demed	demen	demde	demed
	fremman	fremede	fremed	fremmen	fremede	fremed
II.	ian	ode	od	en	ede	ed
	lufian	lufode	lufod	luf(i)en	lufede	lufed
III.	habben	haefde	haefd	habben	hafde, hadde	haved
				haven		had

(48.1) There is great confusion in the classification of weak
verbs in M.E. The endings of the three O.E. classes lose their
distinction in M.E., and it is therefore necessary to make new
divisions. The M.E. verbs may be divided into two classes:
(1) those which form their preterite in -ede and the P.P. in ed;
(2) those which formed their preterite by adding -de or te
directly to the stem. The first group consists of O.E. first
class verbs. The second group consists of the rest of the first
class, and the verbs of the third class.

However, there is levelling even between these two
groups, for one verb may have variant forms; e.g. haefde appears
in M.E. texts variously as hafde, hadde, or havede.

This table shows the necessity for new classifications
because of the confusion in older endings. The weakening of o
to e does away with the difference between the preterite ending
of verbs with geminated consonant of class I, and those of class

II. The simplification of the double consonant in class III
causes this class to fall in with the single consonant stems
of class I.

(49) The conjugation of the M.E. verbs <u>driven</u> and <u>demen</u> ill
serve as a pattern for all M.E. verbs. The forms given are E.Mid.

		<u>Strong</u>		<u>eak</u>	
		Present			
		O.E. Indicative.	M.E.	O.L.	M.E.
Sing.	1.	drife	drive	deme	deme
	2.	drifest,drifst	drivest,drifst	demest,demst	demest,demst
	3.	drifeþ	driveþ	demeþ,demþ	demeþ,demþ
Plur.		drifaþ	driveþ	demaþ	demeþ
		Subjunctive			
Sing.		drive	drive	deme	deme
Plur.		drifen	driven	demen	demen
		Imperative			
Sing.	2.	drif	drif	dem	dem
Plur.	2.	drifaþ	driveþ	demaþ	demeþ
		Infinitive			
		drifan	driven	deman	demen
		Pres. Part.			
		drifende	drivende,drivin	demende	demende,demin
		Preterite			
		Indicative			
Sing.	1.	draf	drof	demde	demde
	2.	drife	drive	demdest	demdest
	3.	draf	drof	dende	demde
Plur.		drifon	driven	demdon	demden
		Subjunctive			
Sing.		drife	drive	demde	demde
Plur.		drifen	driven	demden	demden
		Past Part.			
		drifen	driven	demed	demed

It will be seen from these conjugations that the only
difference between the strong and the weak verb is in the

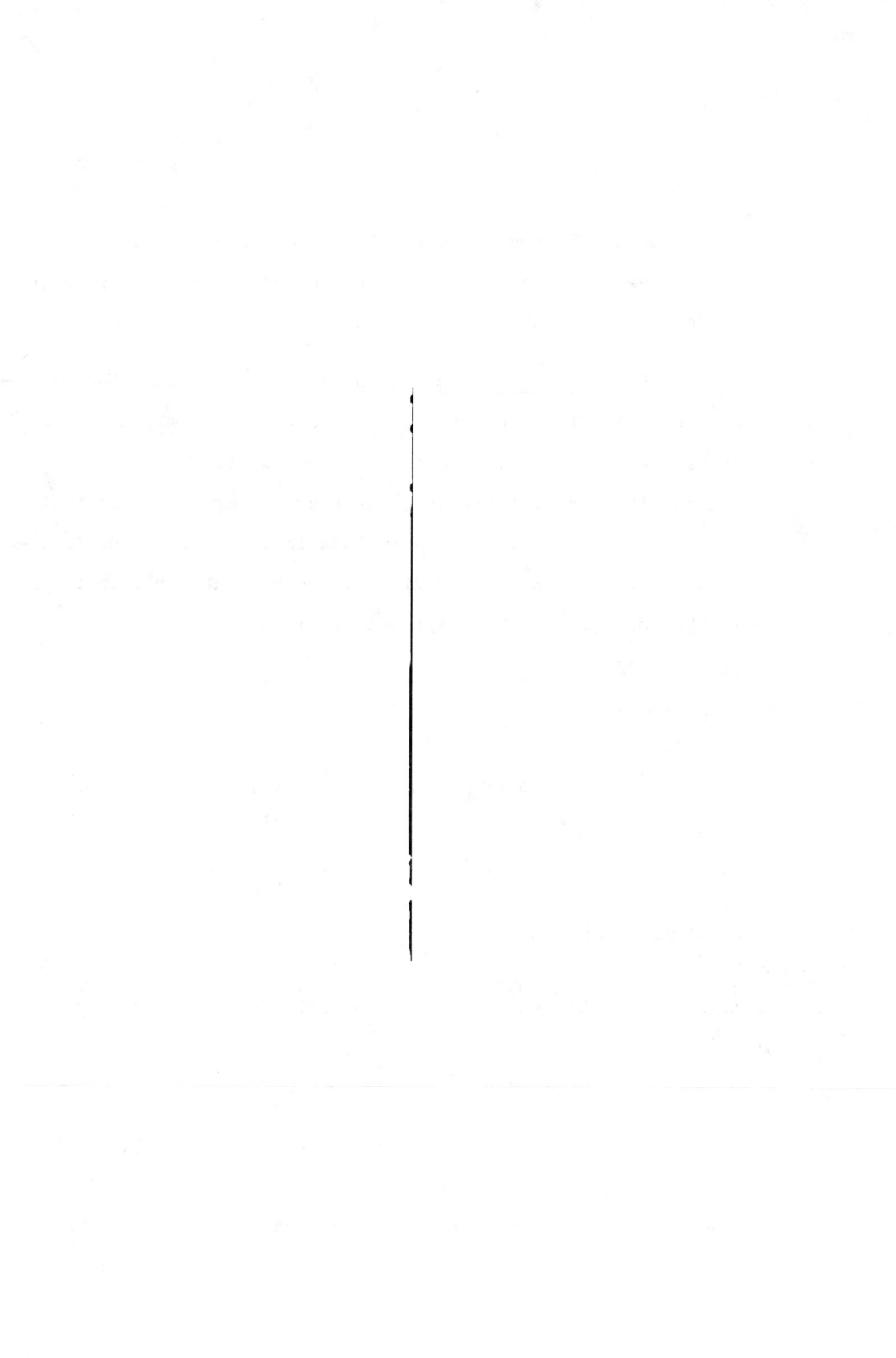

formation of the preterite and in the endings of the preterite
indicative singular. It will also be seen that '.E. weakening
tended to lessen the number of forms in the conjugation.

(50) <u>Dialectal variations.</u> As usual, wherever the obscure vowel
of the inflections occurs, it has the variant spellings of <u>e/i</u>
in Nth. and of <u>e/u</u> in WMid. However, apart from these
common dialectal differences, there are others peculiar to the
verbs. The most noteable variations in the verbs occur in the
present tense - in the infinitive, the present participle, and
in the conjugation of the present indicative.   *82

<u>C.l. bindan</u>

<u>Infinitive</u>

Nth.	WMid	SMid.	SE. Kt.
bind	bind(e)(n)	binde(n)	binden

<u>Present participle</u>

bindand	bindende, bindinge bindand(N.E.)	bindende, bindinde bindinde bindinge	

I   <u>Present indicative</u>

I.binde	binde	binde	binde
2.bindes/is	bindes	bindes/est	bindest
3.bindes/is	bindeþ/es	bindeþ/es	bindeþ

<u>Plural</u>

bindes/is	binden/es	bindes/en bindus/un	þindeþ

(51) <u>Irregular Verbs.</u> The forms of these verbs will be given
in the WMid. dialect. There is one group within these irregular
verbs which can be treated together; apart from this group,

there are four verbs to be considered - be, will, go, an. o.
(51.1) The Preterite present verbs. These verbs belonged to
one or other of the seven classes of strong verbs, and show the
vowels of the preterite of their respective classes in the
present tense. The preterites are weak. In M.., there is little
change peculiar to these verbs beyond a decrease in number.
There are seven important verbs in this group: witen (know),
cunnen (know, be able), durren (dare), shulen (be under obligation, be about to), muwen (be able), moten (be permitted, be
under obligation), and owen (own, be under obligation). The
following are the conjugations of these verbs in the classes to
which they originally belonged: *83

	I. witen	III. cunnen	durren	IV. shulen
Pres.				
Sing. 1.	wōt	can	dar	shal
2.	wūst/wōst	canst	darst	shalt
3.	wōt	can	dar	shal
Plur.	witen	cunnen	dor/dar	shulen
Pret.				
Sing. 1.	wiste	cuþe	durste, dirste	sholde
Plur.	isten	cuþen	dursten	sholden
P.P.	wist	cuþ		

	V. muwen	VI. moten	VII. Owen
Prs.			
Sing. 1.	mai/may	mōt	ōwe
2.	maist/mayst	mōst	ōwest
3.	mai/may	mot	ōwe
Plur.	mowen	mōten	ōwen
Pret.			
Sing. 1.	mihte, michte	mōste	ouhte, oughte
	miȝhte, mighte		
Plur.	mihten, muhten	ōsten	ouhten, oughten

(51.2) The irregular verbs be, will, do and go. [*24]

	bēn		willen	dōn	ōn
Present					
Indic. Sing.					
1.	am/em	þē	.il/wol/wulle	dō	.ō
2.	art	bist/bēst	ilt/ olt/.ult	dōst	.ōst
3.	is	biþ/beþ	il/ ol/ ul	dōþ	.ōþ
Plur.	are(n)/arn	bēn/ beþ	.illeþ/ ilen	.ōn	.ōn
			wulleþ/ .ulen		
Pres. Part.				.ōende, doing	.o.nde, doing.
Pret. Sing. 1.	was/wes		wolde/.ulde	dide,	ʒede, ente
2.	were/wore		.oldest/ .uldest	.idest/dides	ʒeuent, entest
3.	as/was		wolde/.ulde	dide	ʒede, ente
Plur.	eren/woren		.olden/.ulden	.iden	ʒeuen, wenten
Past Part.	ben		wold(e)	don/do	.on

88

CHAPTER XIV

Accidence; Syntax

(52)   The loss of inflections had a far reaching effect on
M.E. syntax. In the first place, it was responsible for the
most obvious difference between O.E. and M.E. syntax in the
change of word order. O.E. was a highly inflected language and
therefore the word order was pliable, but in M.E., it became
necessary to develop a logical word order and to bind the modi-
fiers as closely as possible to the words which they modified.
(52.1) One peculiarity of O.E. word order lay in the frequent
inversion of the subject: gefor AEþered cyning. This peculiarity may also be seen in early M.E. texts, but gradually it
gives place to the logical order of subject and verb so that this
sentence would probably appear as: Ethered the king died. [85]
(52.2) The loss of inflections also resulted in the free use of
the definite article and other demonstratives. M.E. often
omits the article: Beowulf maþelode, bearn Ecgþeowes. However,
in M.E., the article comes to be used before a singular noun in
the 13th century, and by the 14th century it is becoming general
before all nouns. The quotation might have appeared in M.E. as:
Beowulf, the son of Ecgthe . [86]
(52.3) With the loss of inflections in article and adjective
came the further loss of grammatical gender and the adoption of
natural gender. Moreover, when the adjectival inflection was

reduced to e, agreement between nouns and adjectives as to
number and case was lost.   *87

(52.4)   The widespread use of prepositions in M.E. is one
of the most remarkable developments in the language.*88   In
O.E. the prepositions governed certain cases - the genitive,
dative or accusative, but in M.E. they are used with any cases.
The great syntactical development in the 12th century was the
disappearance of the dative case, and the substitution of a
preposition with the nominative-accusative case. During this
century also, the preposition of comes to be used more and more
frequently in place of the old genitive case.
O.E. goldwine gumena sprae c mildum wordum, would take a different
form in M.E.: - the gold-friend of men spoke with mild words.
(52.5)   In O.E., the subject of a verb was frequently unex-
pressed, but in M.E., with the weakening of verbal endings, the
expressed subject became a strict necessity.
O.E. bugon to bence ould be expressed in M.E. - they bent to
        the bench.

        It is to be noted that all of these changes, dependent
upon the weakening of inflections ould, of necessity, not become
general until L.M.E.

(53)   Apart from the changes in syntax due to loss of inflections are certain other features of th   ... syntax hich
deserve note.

90

(53.1)   Lven in O.E., the impersonal construction with
hit as the subject was familiar, but this particular construction gained favor in the M.L. period. Huchon suggests
that the frequency with which it occurs may be due to French
influence. *89

(53.2)   The old interrogatives in the Nom.,Accus.,Gen., and
Dat., cases take the place of earlier relatives in M.L. The
The forms become N.E. who, whom, whose, which. *90

(53.3)   The O.E. method of comparison of adjectives by the
addition of the -er, -est, suffixes was retained in M.E., but
beside it a new formation became more and more frequent.
This was the use of the forms more and most with the positive.
Huchon suggests that this, also may be the result of French
influence. *91

(53.4)   O.E. and early M.E. both expressed a negative with
a double form. This practice began to disappear in M.L., and
particularly in the north, the single negative began to be
used in the 14th century.*92

(54)   Owing to the general inflectional confusion throughout the period, it is not unusual to find an article and
modifier in the Nom. while the noun is in the Dat., or to
find verbs and their subjects disagreeing in number or even
person, but these irregularities are not to be taken as the
usual practice or as illustrative of any law of syntax in . .

91

CHAPTER XV

Borrowings

(55)   The borrowings in M.E. come chiefly from two sources,
Scandinavian and French. The influence of these languages can
be seen in three fields: in orthography, in accidence, and
in vocabulary.

(56)   Scandinavian influence. There is no evidence of any
great orthnographical changes due to Scandinavian influence.
The effect of the Scandinavian language upon M.E. can be best
seen in the northern dialects, for it was here that the great
influx of Northmen occurred.

(56.1) Accidence. The general effect of Norse upon the system
of accidence was its contribution to the rapid breaking down
of the inflections. The extent of this influence may be gauged
in comparing the radical loss of inflections in the north with
the conservative retention of them in the south. *93

The more particular instances of Norse influence are
those connected with the third person pronoun. The new forms,
thei, theim, and their, were developed from the Norse forms,
þeir þeira, þeim. The new forms ere adopted in M.E. first
in the Mid. and North, and slowly spread to the south. *94

(56.2) Vocabulary. The general nature of the Scandinavian
borrowings was a distinctly domestic one.   They were terms of

everyday use of the common people, and were very numerous in
Nth. and the Mid. dialects. Some N.E.words which came into
the language from the Norse this time are: knife, fellow, egg,
husband, skin, skirt, etc.

It is often very difficult to distinguish those words
of Norse origin, which had cognate forms in English - e.g.
M.E. grai from O.N. grā, beside M.E. grei, from O.E. græg -
Norse borrowings were often simple synonyms for ordinary
English words - e.g. sky from O.N. beside heaven from O.E.

However, there are certain cases in which the O.N.
origin may be clearly detected. One group of these words are
those beginning with <u>sk</u>. The O.E. <u>sc</u> became the ($\int$) written
<u>sh</u> sound, but the O.N. <u>sk</u> had an explosive value which it re-
tained, written <u>sk</u>. or <u>sch</u>. Among such words are: skill,
school, busk, skip. [95]

Another group is composed of the patronymics ending in
-<u>son</u>. Thomson, Johnson, Mosson Mill are examples of this. Then,
in the north there are many towns and villages with the suffixe
-by, thorp, toft, thwaite, all of which are Norse suffixes
meaning 'village': Whitby, Grimsby, Weaverthorpe, Fridaythorpe,
Armathwaite, Lowestoft, Slaithwaite.[96]

Words which have (g) or (k) where English words have (j)
or ($t\int$) -- i.e. infront positions - are usually of Norse
origin: gift, get, leg, rig, kirk (O.E. chiriche).

93

The development of ā and āe is different in the t o
lan_ua_es. In M.E., ā remained in Nth., and became ō elsewhere. In O.N. it became ai. See raid beside road (M.E.
development): āe became ē in M..., but ei in O.N., see ..
_rei beside grai.

In M.., Norse loan words could sometimes be recognised by a diphthong where the English form had a simple
vowel: blak beside bleik.

(57) French Influence. French, at first in the Anglo-
Norman dialect, came in with William the Conqueror, and was
the language of the aristocracy and the educated classes until
the late 14th and early 15th centuries. So profound was its
influence that it was retained as the proper parliamentary
language until well on into the sixteenth century, while in
the law courts it was not ousted officially until 1731, and
even then many French law terms were retained. [97]

(57.1) Orthography. The influence of the A.-N. scribes was
a very extensive one in M.E. [98] Not only did they aid in the
disappearance of characteristic O.E. symbols, but they introduced many of their own symbols into native words. The French
symbols introduced to express M.E. vowel sounds were the
following: ie for ē, diep to express dēp; occasionally o for u,
foll for full; ou for ū, hous for . . hūs; and u for long or
short y, burie for . . būriʒ . There were also new symbols
among the consonants: ch was used to express M.E. front c;

child for C.E. cild; French qu was adopted or O.L. cw, quen
in place of cwen; voiceless s was expressed in the French
manner by c before e or i, certain, cite; na in early .L.,
the ($\int$) sound was written ss by French writers.

(57.2)   <u>Accidence.</u> The effect of the French tongue was
not nearly as great as that of the Norse in this branch, but
there are a few details worth noting in the syntax. The great
frequency with which the impersonal construction is used in
M.E. would seem to point to French influence; the new method of
the comparison of adjectives with more and most would seem to
point even more definitely to French influence; and occasional
constructions such as - a so grete man - reflect the peculiarities of French syntax. [*99]

(57.3)   <u>Vocabulary</u> There are certain suffixes which
indicate French origin, and among these are; -ice, -ience,
-age, as they appear in 'justice', 'patience', 'dalliance',
'corage'. A very large number of these abstract nouns ere
borrowed during the N.L. period.

        Many terms describing Arthur and his chivalrous
knights were borrowed from the French: corteisie, chevalry,
gentyle, gracios.

        The terms describing the rich materi l ich were
being newly imported were French: sendal, tolouse, selure,
pelure. (See Gawayne and the Grene Knight).

95

A number of words describing food were borrowed at
this period. Prominent among these are the terms for cooked
meats as distinct from the names of the living animals: beef,
mutton, veal, etc.

Until well on in the 14th century, when a semblance
of a literary dialect appears, the greater number of French
borrowings are to be found in the south, where the court was
held and where the Anglo-Normans settled. This differentiation in vocabulary is yet another means of distinguishing one
dialect from another.

(58)   There are some minor groups of borrowings from other
languages. The proximity of Wales, and the great interest in
the Celtic romances were responsible for the introduction of a
number of Celtic words. [101] Many of them were place names,
but there are a few others such as <u>bodkin</u> and <u>clan</u>. Again the
great body of translations from the Latin [102] had a considerable effect upon the vocabulary: cause, diligent, crucify,
lunatic - ~~luick~~.

Trade with the low countries and an influx of Flemish
weavers probably helped to add Dutch words like <u>jerkin</u>,
<u>hogshead</u>. [103]

THE LANGUAGE OF CHAUCER

(59)   The language of Chaucer was representative of the
London dialect of his day, which will be further discussed in
Chapter XVII, and was predominantly E.Mid. with, however, a
fairly large southern element.[104] Chaucer's pronunciation is
deduced, partly from his orthography, partly from his rhymes,
and partly from the analogy of other dialects, but such
deductions are only approximate.

(60) _Phonology._   Variant forms in Chaucer show developments
from the dialectal peculiarities which made up the differences
between Angl. and W.S. in O.E. For instance, the two vowels
which develop from P.O.E. āe(ē: in Mid., and ɛ: in W.S.) both
appear in Chaucer in the same word[105] e.g. O.E. dǣd ary ears
as (dɛ:d), (de:d). Chaucer also shows the W.S. developments
from forms with breaking in W.S. but not in Angl.[106] O.E. ac ld
appears both as cold (from W.S. cald with lengthening) and as
oold (from Angl. ald with lengthening).

(60.1) _Lengthening and Shortening._   Chaucer shows a tendency to
retain the results of O.E. lengthening (see note to 14) before
ld, nd, mb in such forms as childe, kinde, comb, which all have
long vowels. Also, before these consonant groups, original
long vowels are frequently retained as in heeld and foend.[107]
M.E. lengthening of a short vowel in an open accented syllable
is obvious in such words as maken (a:) and f_rlore (ɔ:)

     Except in the case of vowels before consonant groups

noted above, W.S. shortening ap ears to have acted n rmally.
(60.8) Simple Vowels. Amon the vowels whic' ere n m lly
unc'an ed in W.S. (see 18), there are cer'ain interestin forms
in C'aucer. In the case of a/o before a nasal, t ere is a stron
ten'e cy to use o before the groups nd, ng, mb but a elsewhere:
lomb and an. *108   The spelling womman (with o for u before m)
shows the characteristic L.O.S. rounding of i to (y) after w,
which ws retained in S.W. *109

       The O.W. vowels ắ, āē, ū, ō, ẏ and ȳ shows the
developments:
ắ always ap ears as a, the normal Mid. development; pacf --path
āē shows the usual Midl, and S.W. chan e to (ɛ:); dāē l--(d ɛ :l)
ā usually has the southern chan_e to (ɔ:), but so etimes, in
con ection with wh or w, t ere is a variation between (ɔ:) and (o:) *110
       O.W. hwā-- (hw/ɔ:) or (hwo:)
ō remains as (o:) O... bōe--(bo:k)
ẏ shows t'ree dialectal developments; [111] e(showing t'e St. chan e
of y to e) is the most frequent; i (the n r al Mid. development
is also frequent)
while u (sh wing t'e S.W. chan e) is rare. O. . l st ap ears s
list, lest, lyst.
       O... synne ap ears as senne or sinne, O. . b r en ap ears
           burden.
ȳ has t'e Mid. develo ent to i, alt ' ce i n lly t.
       e ap ears;
       O... fȳr--(fi:r) or (fe:r).

98

(60.3) _Diphthongs._   Developments from O.E. diphthongs show
some departures from E.Mid. also. Long and short ea show the
normal changes to (ε:) and _a_ respectively. Long and short
eo show the E.Mid. change to (e:) and e, but some forms
suggest a variant development to E.E. ($\emptyset$) after w. [112]
O.E. sweord appears as swerd or sword.

Developments from N.E. long and short ie show again the
influence of that dialect. O.E. hierde--hirde.

The new diphthongs arising in M.E. appear normally in
Chaucer (see Chapter VIII). However, where an ai diphthong
has developed from an earlier ei diphthong, Chaucer writes
it ei: [113]   grei becomes later grai, but is written by Chaucer
grei.

(60.4) _Consonants._ Generally speaking, the consonants in
Chaucer follow the regular developments of consonants in M.E.,
and particularly those in E.Mid. [114] although there are a few
instances of the influence of other dialects.

Vocalisation. The vocalisation of $\math;3$ to i and of w to u
medially between vowels or finally after, occurs regularly.

O.E. we$\math;3$--wey, way; O.E. feowere--foure.

Assimilation. The assimilations which occur generally in
M.E. are evident in Chaucer--O.E. at ƿo --atto(see 32,3)

Disappearance of consonants. The M.E. disappearance of
unstressed ch, k,l,n,v and w is evidenced in Chaucer, although
in the case of l and w there are variant forms which suggest
further influence. [115]

99

M.E. ich --I; L.M.E. make ɡe--maad; M.I.E. min--my;
E.M.E. loverd--lord, but O.E. swylc appears in Chaucer as
either sich (M'id.) or swich (with a characteristic Nth.
retention of w); also,hwylc appears as whylk.

Inserted consonants. b was inserted after m-thombe; d
was inserted between l and r-thonder, and p was often inserted
between m and n-solempne.

Isolative changes. f, v s followed the usual development
of these consonants in L.Mid. except for the fact that,
occasionally, f appears to be voiced initially, due to Kt.
influence, as in vixen. [*116]

Sc also followed the regular development to (ʃ)
except medially before and finally after a back vowel where it
became, in all dialects, (sk) [*117]
O.E. scip --ship; O.E. dusc--dusk.

The two values of c usually developed normally according
to L.Mid..Front c became (tʃ), and back c became (k). [*118]
However, there are a few instances of k where (tʃ) is expected.
O.E. benc--bench; O.E. caru--care (k); but O.E. mycel appears
as mikel or muchel (the k here is probably due to Nth. influence, here the k was adopted from the O.N. cognate, ikill).

ȝ Most c normal developments in its various
positions. [*119] The back explosive became (dȝ), bridȝe
(bridȝə); the medial back continuant l biclised to and
vocalised to u, dawes (d uəs); while the initial front

continuant remained written y as in ycer, and medial and
final front continuant ȝ developed a glide and vocalised to
form a diphthong, as in sai.

h disappeared initially before liquids or nasals and
in some instressed words; nute from hnutu, and it or hit from
hit. Medially and finally, h became a continuant (χ)
spelled gh, laughter and knyght, [*120]

Weakening in unstressed syllables. Long vowels in prefixes shortened regularly; ārisen became ărisen. Unstressed
monosyllables also shortened and, where there was a final n,
this often disappeared; O.E. ān became a (n). In the inflectional syllables, the indeterminate vowel (ə) was usually written e,
although there are occasional i forms in Chaucer, used for the
sake of rhyme; werkes or werkis.

Final (ə) [*121] This vowel was tending to disappear in
Chaucer's day, much more rapidly in the North than in the South,
but it did not go completely until the end of the 15th century.
When Chaucer needed an extra syllable in rhyme, he often sounded
the (ə) where, otherwise, it would have disappeared. In the
following positions, (ə) normally was silent; in the pronominal forms, hire, oure, thyne, etc.; in the plurals, thise,
some, ecche; in the 2nd sing. pret. of strong verbs, bade;
in the P.P. of strong verbs with a short root when the final n
had disappeared, rite; and in such words as before, the, here.
Otherwise, there seems to have been a rough rule that final (ə)
was elided before a vowel or an h.

101

The <u>nouns and adjectives</u> in Chaucer show a strong
tendency towards the conservative declensions of S. . *102
In the singular of nouns, the indeterminate (ə) ending is
found where this would have disappeared in E.Mid. However,
where it is necessary for rhyme or metre, Chaucer often uses
the E.Mid. form without ending. Hence, both fyre and fyr are
found. The old -r declension gen. sing. is sometimes found as
in 'brother wif'; and occasionally this ending is seen in other
declensions, e.g. his lady grace.

In the plurals of nouns, Chaucer normally uses the
southern -en ending, although this is often found side by side
with the Mid. -es ending; namen or names. The <u>adjectives</u>
have the usual strong and weak forms in .. . The general developments of both nouns and adjectives in Chaucer agree with the
normal M.E. changes (see Chapter XI).

The <u>pronouns</u> have regular southern forms except for she and
they, which are Mid. forms (see further Chapter XII).

In the <u>verbs</u>, Chaucer generally uses southern forms. *103
The infinitive normally ends in -en, although there are frequent
instances of the disappearance of final -n, fallen or falle.
In the singular pres,, he uses southern forth in the third
person, although in the pres. plur. he uses Mid. -n; falleth,
and fallen. The pres, part. es the Mid. or in -ing(e) as in
fallinge. (See Chapter XIII for the . . forms).

<u>Orthography</u>. *104 As a rule, the long vowels are indicated

by a double symbol: (e:) is spelled ee, and (o:) is spelled oo.
However, (u:) is written ou. The consonants are almost entirely written in the normal Mid. and S.W. symbols. F and th
exist together. The spelling sal for shal is to be noted, for
it might indicate Kt. or even Nth. influence.

     <u>Vocabulary.</u> *125 Chaucer's vocabulary is largely
made up of English and French words which were in common use
during his day. Huchon points out that, in the poems, there
are not above thirty words which cannot be found in much earlier
texts. In the prose, however, there is a large body of
borrowings by reason of the fact that most of the prose work is
direct translation. It is in the prose work also that a reason-
ably large number of learned Latin words occurs, but these,
again, are pressed into the service of translation. Chaucer
does not use them elsewhere.

     There are practically no Scandinavian terms in the
vocabulary. This, coupled with the fact that Chaucer does not
use archaic English words, helps to explain why Chaucer's poems
are so much easier to read than are "Sir Gawayne and the Grene
Knight" or "The Vision of Piers Plowman" which are more or
less contemporary with him.

     <u>Non-Mid. features.</u> A curious form is an occasional
ar from O.E. eor, where the normal E.Mid. form would be er, and
the normal S. form would be (ø). *126 It would seem that
there was an occasional retraction of the er to ar even in . .

although it did not become at all general until early N.E.
O.E. deorc -- N.E. derk, l.N.E. dark (rare)

There is a slight element of Nth. in Chaucer.
It appears in forms such as han and wha, which show the Nt
retention of a instead of the normal Mid. and Sth. develop
ment to (∂ :) The Nth. element also appears in swylk and
whylk beside the southern forms sich[such and which, with
disappearance of l.

The strongest evidence of Kt. influence is seen
in a form like evil, which shows the characteristic Kt. de
opment of O.E. y to e.

In accidence, the influence of S.W. is particul
strong, although it can also be seen in the lack of Scandi
forms in the vocabulary.

CHAPTER   XVII

Literary Tendencies in M.E.

(70)   The rise of a literary dialect.

The London dialect of E.Mid. became the literary
dialect of English by the end of the 14th century. In the O.L.
period, the W.S. dialect became the literary dialect for that
time but, after the coming of the Normans, this literary supremacy was destroyed and, during the greater part of the M.L.
period there was no one literary dialect. Towards the end of
the period, there was a change. In the 14th century, there was
a growing tendency for E.Mid. forms to penetrate into southern
writings until, in the second half of the century, such writings
were almost wholly E.Mid. in character. That is, the London
dialect of the late 14th century had become predominantly E.Mid.

        This change had been effected by the time of Chaucer,
Wyclif, Gower and their contemporaries, who wrote in the
dialect of London. It is through their influence that London
E.Mid. becomes the literary dialect of the English language.[1-7]
Indeed, Chaucer and Wyclif may be called the creators of our
literary language for it was through their popularity, appealing
as they did to various sections and classes of the country that
the necessary impetus was given to the growing literary supremacy
of London E.Mid. Ten Brink says ' Wyclif prepared great masses
of the people for the reception of a common literary language,

the norral form in ea ly texts is the eo or o spelling,
indicating the rounded o ($\emptyset$). Beside this type, up until the
14th century, there is also the e type from `id., and the ie
type from Kt. From the beginning of the 14th century on, the
Mid.e is the only form. [129]

O.E. y has a more divided development. [130] Both the
S.W. u and the !id. i are found throughout the period, and
in the 14th century, Kt. e forms are added.

In accidence, the conservatism of the south and S.E.Mid.
is evident. Only one of the new third person pronouns is used
 ith any frequency until the late 14th century. Only Fei or
thei occurs in the 13th and early 14th centuries. [131] In the
verbs, the -eth of the third pers. sing. is retained throughout
the period, but the Mid. -en or -e for the plur. pres. is
common beside the southern -e F in the 13th and early 14th
centuries, and finally becomes the uniform ending in the late
14th. The strongest evidence of Mid. influence in the verbs is
to be seen in the pres. part. [132] Throughout the 13th century,
the -ende of the Mid. appears beside the characteristically
southern -inde, but in the 14th century, the southern form is
ousted altogether by the new `id. -ing ending.

Thus, by the end of the 14th century, nearly all of
the purely southern elements had disappeared, and even here
they remained, they had id. variants.

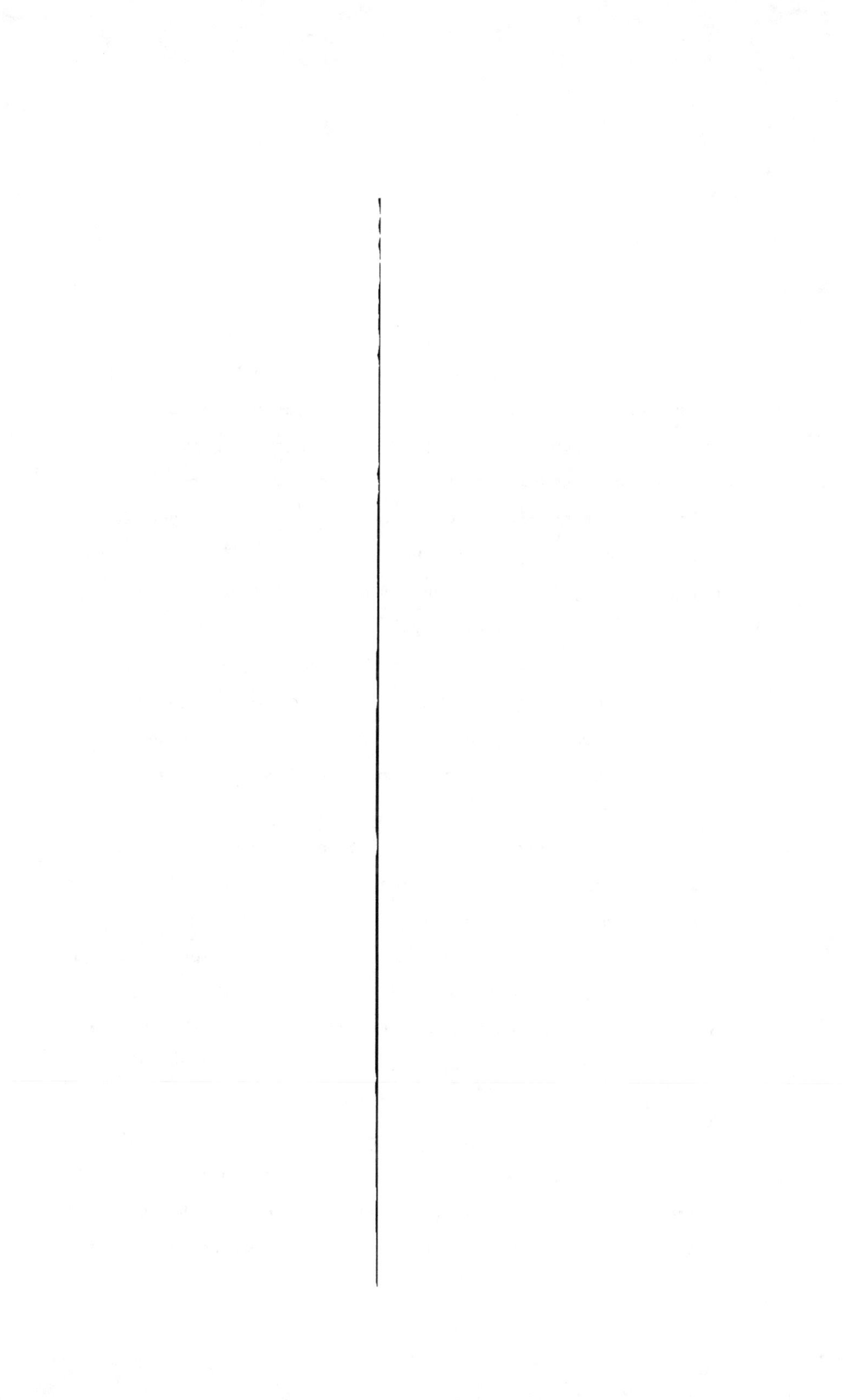

(72)   <u>Alliterative poetry in the '.E. period.</u>

In O..., there were five types of alliterative line, as postulated by Sievers. By the I'.E. period, two of these - the D and E types - had already disappeared largely because the poetic compounds, characteristic of O.E. poetry, upon which they depended, had disappeared.[133] The C.type, A//A, was much less frequent for the same reason.[134] The two remaining types, A and B, were affected by the '.E. sound changes in an interesting way.

The A type was by far the most frequent in O.E. alliterative poetry.[135] This was fairly naturel in an inflected language, for the rhythm / X / A fits a language in which the weaker part of the word comes last. However, during the I'.E. period, the inflectional endings gradually disappeared, and so the tendency in rhythm was toward the B type A / A /.[136] This tendency was strengthened by the necessary introduction of prepositions to take the place of the lost endings.[137]

That is, the loss of the O.E. inflectional endings largely caused the shifting from a falling rhythm to a rising one, from trochaic to iambic. This shift is possibly the most important and certainly the most fundamental difference between Old and Modern English verse.[138]

There was another temporal effect owing to the loss of endings. The number of monosyllabic words was greatly increased, and it affected, not only the verse, but the whole field of literary expression for a time, producing the

108

Other ".E. changes also showed their influence upon the
alliterative verse. Lengthening helped to cause the disappearance of the resolved stress of '.... poetry, *159
while the action of the shortening,*140 especially in
increased the number of thesis syllables, and generally helped
to break down the definite forms of U.... poetry and lead to a
vague formless rhythm in '.E. poetry.*141 On the other hand,
shortening contributed greatly to the quickening of movement
in '.E. poetry which is a very striking difference between
O.E. and ".E. alliterative verse. Moreover, it was through
shortening that the time element of O.E. poetry was lost.*142

With shortening, English verse became purely accentual,
and so the accentual rhythms of the continent were introduced
the more easily.

(73)   Types of Literature in the '.... Period.

In quantity, the religious, moral and didactic writings
of the '.E. period are foremost. In the 10th century they are
the only considerable body, but in the 11th century, there is
an amazing outcropping of romances and social writings which
were well supported by the tales, lyrics, chronicles and plays
of the period. Naturally, we cannot judge precisely of the
literary output of any one dialect at any period for the
simple reason that many writings must have been destroyed, but
the writings which have been preserved enable us to generalize

on the tendencies of the three centuries, and to judge of
the proportionate literary strength of the various dialects.
(73.1)   The 12th century seems to have been a particularly
unproductive one, and only a few scattered writings have come
down to us. The 13th century shows a substantial increase,
and the 14th century gives us a really considerable body of
prose and poetry.

The division of the writings into dialects is most
enlightening. In the 12th century, there is very little
difference between one or another. In the 13th, it is interesting to note that, as far as quantity goes, the S. . dialect
keeps the place which it held in O... as the predominant
literary dialect. However, W.Mid. shows a rapidly increasing
group of writings; L.Mid. and Kt. are more or less equal, ith
E. Mid. leading slightly; Nth. has the smallest group. The
situation is considerably changed in the 14th century. The
tremendous literary energy of Nth. and the id. dialects completely overshadows the waning interest in S. . and the few
productions in Kt.
(73.2)   The type of literature which was produced during the
M.E. period also throws revealing light on the intervals of
the different centuries and dialects. The <u>romances</u> have a
slight beginning in the id. and southern dialects in the 13th
century, but at that time there were apparently none in Nth.
This fact throws into greater prominence their popularity in

110

Nth. in the 14th century. The strong spirit of <u>social satire</u>
in Mid. and Nth. which gave rise to many writings concerning
contemporary conditions in the 14th century, seems to be lacking in S.W. and Kt. In Nth., side by side with the keen interest in romances, there is an awakening of <u>religious con-
sciousness</u> in the 14th century. This spirit seems to be
stronger in Nth. than in any other dialect in the century, though
it was more prominent in S.W. and W.Mid. in the previous century.
Perhaps the greatest body of <u>lyrics</u> in any one dialect is to
be found in S.W. of the 13th century, when there were a number
of collections. The lyrical interest seems to die away in S.W.
during the 14th century, although it increases in most of the
other dialects. Perhaps one of the most outstanding additions
to the literature of the 14th century is the appearance of
several collections of <u>plays</u>. We know that a certain amount
of religious drama existed before the 14th century,[*143] and
it is evident that most of the plays which do appear then are
based on older originals, but the very fact that they were
collected in the 14th century shows that there must have been
a growing interest in drama, and a growing realisation of the
importance of the existing plays.

(74)   The chart which follows has been compiled largely from
Well's "Manual of M.E. Writings', and the writings have been
classified according to his system except for the fact that

several of his smaller divisions such as roverbs, iblical
translations, the works of ycliffe an his follo ers -
have all been included uner 'Religious nd iaactic ritin s'.
 here yld differs from ells as to at an dialect yld's
decision has been taken. *144

CHART OF M.E. PERIODS

12th Century.

Romances Tales Chronicles Social Religious Dialogues Science *

Nth.   Nothing in Northern   Lyrics

                                                                             Drama

E. MID.   orcester
                                     Cathedral
                                     Fragments

W. MID.   Peterborough
            Chronicle
                                                 Trinity
                                                 College
                                                 Homilies

S.W.   *Herbarium
                                                               Apuleii

Kt.   Kentish
                                     Gospels

                                     Kentish
                                     Homilies

Romances	Tales	Chronicles	Social	Religious	Dialogues	Science	Lyrics	Drama
			A Ballad	Scottish Coll.				
			on the	of Legends				
			Scottish	Northern				
			Wars	Metrical				
				Psalter				
Sir		Lagamon A	Land of	Wooing of				
Tristrem			Cockayne	our Lord				
				A Lutel				
		Lagamon B (Har.915)		Booth Sermon			Tanner	
				Catherine			169	
				Group				
				Ancren Riwle				
				God Ureisun				
				Sawles Ward				
				Compassio				
				Mariae				
				Doomsday				
				Jacob &				
				Joseph				
				Sayings of				
				St. Bernard				
				On Serving				
				Christ				
				Southern				
				Legendary				
				DEATH				

13th Century

Romances	Tales	Chronicles	Social	Religious	Dialogues	Science	Lyrics	Drama
King Horn Floris and Blancheflour Havelock	Bestiary			Ormulum Proverbs of Hendyng Genesis & Exodus La Estoire del Evangelie	Bet. the Virgin & the Cross	Prog. of Popular Science	Stations of Rome	Rawlinson G.22 Arundel 292
Bevis of Hamtoun	The Fox & the Wolf Dame Siriz		Hwon oly Chireche is under Iote	Poema Morale Holi Maidenhead Cotton Vespasian Homilies Death Assumption of our Lady Fifteen Signs of Judgment Proverbs of Alfred The Passion Maximian A Sarmun	Owl & Nightingale Church & [?]- in ale	Usages of Winchester Proc. of Henry III		Cotton Titus D.VII, 171 Lambeth, 487, 169 Cotton Nero A XI Royal 17 A .VII, 206 Cotton Caligula A I. Jesus Coll., 29 Digby 86 Arundel 45 Trinity Coll., Cbc. B, 14, 39 Digby 2 Harley 978 (Sumer is icumen)
Arthour & Merlin King Alisaunder				Five Lit. Sermons Vices & Virtues Disputation bi-twene Childe Jesus & Maistres of the Lawe of Jesus				

Ywain &
Gawain
Octovian
Awyntrs of
Arthur
Gest Hist-
oriale of
Destruction
of Troy
Sege of
Melayne
Sir Eglamour
Morte Arthure
Sir Percyvelle
Sir Degrevant
Sir Madace
Chevalere
As one
31 Ottuel
Le one
Florence
Avowynge of
Arthur
Nth.

Seven
Sages
of Rome
The Gest
Chronicle
of Cy
The Childe
of Bristowe
(Har.2382)

Thomas Bok
of Castle-
ford's
Chronicle
of England

Barbours
Bruce

The Kings
breaking
of Magna
Carta
Lawrence
Minot's
Songs

Tomas of
Erssel-
doune

Scottish
rophec-
ies

Cursor
Mundi
Lay Folks
Mass Book
Sermo in
Festo Corpor-
is Christi
Surtees
Psalter
Gnomies of Man
Northern
Metrical
Homily Cycle
Richard Rolle
Mirror of St.
Edmund
Commentary
on Matthew,
Mark, Luke.
Dan John
Gaytryges
Sermon
Castel of Love
A.B.C. of Aristotle
Stophic Version
of Old. Test.
Version of Pauline
Epistles
Lay-folks
Catechism
Pistill of Susan
Mirror of Life
Wm. Nassington
Athanasian Creed
Distichs of Cato
Vision of undale

Phillips
Recipes

Rawlinson
Poetry 175

Arundel
507
Harley
1022
Cbg. Univ.
Libr. Dd.
v.64

York Plays

Romances	Tales	Chronicles	Social	Religious	Dialogue	Science	Ly
Sir Orfeo		Short Metri-	Harley	Speculum	Dispute		Har
Sir Degare		cal Hist.	91	Gy of	between		(Alys
Alisaunder A		of England	Parliament	Warewyke	Mary &		Har.
Alexander &		Robt. of	of Three	St. Brandan	the Cross		Roya
Dindimus-B		Gloucester	Ages	Life of			XVII
m. of Palerne		Trevisas	Wynnere &	Thos. Beket			The
Joseph of		Trans. of	Wastour	St. Juliana			Poem
Arimathie		Higdens	Vision of	Walter			Wm E
Song of Roland		Polychro-	Piers Plow-	Hilton			
Sir Gawayne &		nicon	man A & B	Patience			
the Grene Knight			Knyghtons	Purity			
Roberd of Cisyle			Chronicle	The			
Le 'orte Arthur			Vision of	Festival			
Laud-Troy ook			Piers	of John			
			Plowman C	Mirk			
			Richard				
			Redeless				

Romances	Tales	Chronicles	Social	Religious	Dialogue	Science	Ly
Amis &	The remyte	Robt	On the	Meditations	Lament-		M.a
miloun	Outelewe	Tannynge	Evil Times	of the	ation of		Hea
orn	Vernon	of Brunne's	of Ed.II	Passion	Mary		c
Child	Seven Ages	Rimed	Adam Davys	Robt. Mannyng	to		el
Guy of	of Rome	Story of	Dreams of	Hand-Lyng	St. Bernard		
rwick		England	Ed. II	Synne			Sto
Lai le		Short Met-	The Praise	Earliest			ec
Freine		rical	of Women	Complete	Ypotis		ir
Otuel		Chronicle	On the	Eng. Prose			et
in of Tars		of Eng.	Earthquake	Psalter			to
ol nd			of 1382	Pety Iob			lia
Ferumu			Norfolk	Seven			in
uy of arwick			Guilds	Penetential			Lon
Sir Launfal				Psalms			Cha
				Castel of Love			Joc

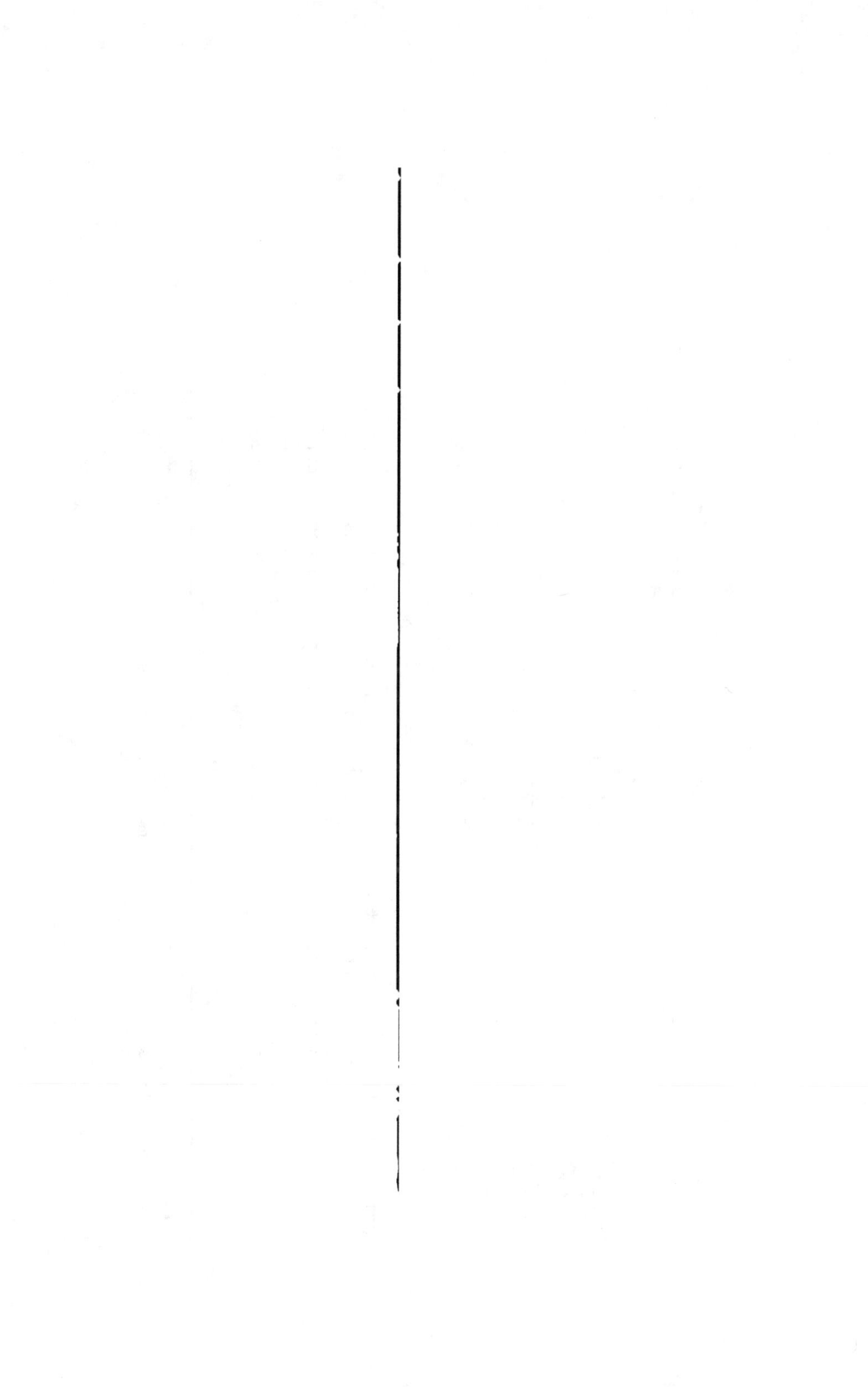

Romances	Tales	Chronicles	Religious	Science	Lyrics	Drama
Libeaus Desconious Tale of Camelyn Octovian Ipomadon Athelston Sir Isumbras Emare Sir Gowther Sowdone of Babylone			Canticum of Creatione Juliana Lampit Wycliffe Osbern Bokenam's Lives of Saints			
Arthur Sir Tirumbras Seege of Troy	Narratio de Virtute Missarum Narratio Sancti Augustini	Sht. Met. Chronicle of England	Mirror of Sinners Smaller Vernon Coll. Form of Confession Ab cy of the Holy Ghost Meditation of the Five Wounds of Christ	Constitutions of Masonry Deed of 1396	Rawlinson D.913 Vernon Simeon	Caiphas Towncley
Richard Coer de Lyons	Seven Sages of Rome		Agenbite of Inwit Wm. of Shorehams Poems		Gower	

ILLUSTRATIONS OF ... DIALECTS ... IN 14th C.....Y

	Nth	..Mld.	..Mld.	..	St.
her heart	her herte	her herte	hur hurte	hor hurte	hare herte
their hearts	thair hertes	hir hertes	hur hurtus	hure hurten	hare herten
foul devils	ful deviles	foul deviles	foul dueveles	voule dueveles	voule dyevelen
deadly sin	dedly sin	dedli sinne	dedli sinne	dedly sunne	dyadelveh senne
to the man	to the man	to þe man	to þe mon	to þo manne	to þane
in a row	in soru	in sorrow	in soru	in sorowe	ino sorȝe
of such kind	of swilk kinde	of siche kinde	suche kunde	of siche kunde	of suyche kende
I will say	I wil sai	I wil seyn	I wol saie	ich wule siggo	ich wyle sig e
she says	scho sais	sche seyth	ho saith	hoo serth	hy say þ
he shall see	he sal se	he shal sen	he shal seen	he schal ise	he ssel yzy
they have	thai have	they have (n)	thai/hy haven	hy habben	hy hab eþ
to show	to scaw	to (s)howe(n)	to showe(n)	sheuen	to ssewy
loving	lovand	lovinge	loving	loviinde	loviynde

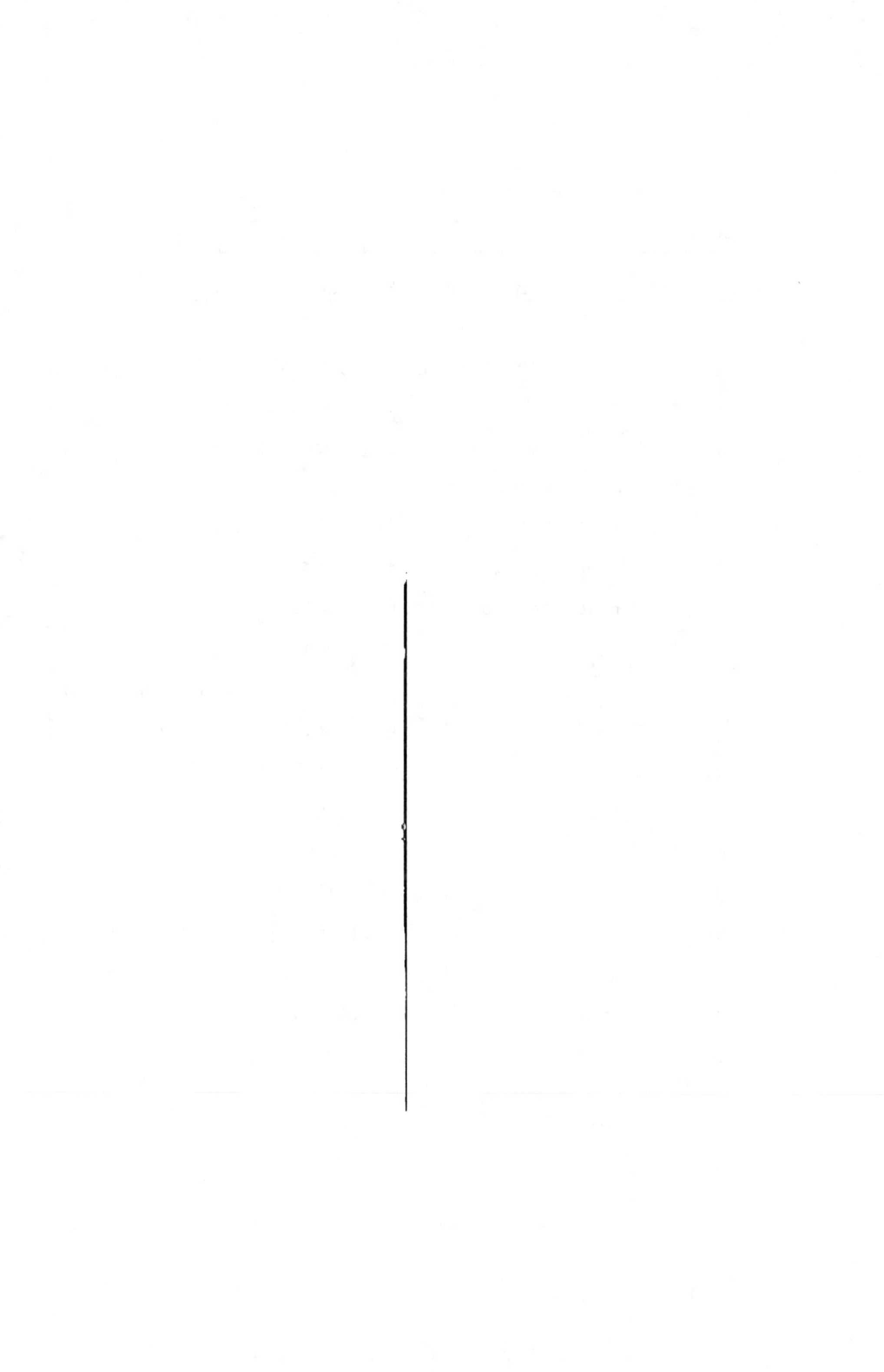

SOUND CHANGES FROM M.E. TO MODERN ENGLISH

The normal developments of M.E. vowel sound in modern English.

. a   as in hat   becomes M.E.   ae   (hae t)

a: "   " name   "   "   o: (no:m)

e   "   " bed   remains "   e   (bed)

e: "   " dep   becomes "   i: (di:p)

ɛ: "   " heal   "   "   i   (hi:l

i   "   " sing   remains "   i   (siŋ)

i: "   " ride   becomes "   ai   (raid)

ə   "   " flok   "   "   ə   or a (flək) or

                                      (flak)- American.

ə: "   " road   "   "   o: (ro:d)

o: "   " bok   "   "   u   (buk)

o: "   ' food   "   "   u: (fu:d)

o: "   " blod   "   "   ʌ   blʌd)

u   "   " buck   "   '   ʌ   (bʌk)

u: "   " hus   "   "   au   (haus)

ai   "   " day   "   "   oi   (doi)

au   "   " draw   "   "   ə: (drə:)

eu   '   " neue   "   '   ju   (nju:)

eu   "   " cheu   "   "   u: (tʃu:)

ou   "   " bowe   '   "   o: (bo:)

ou   "   " bough   "   "   au   (bau)

____

Influence of Consonants on Vowels

(1) f,s,θ

    a + f,s,θ   ā or æ (b ā θ) (ɪɪɡ ɑh) or

                          (b æ θ) (ɑɛɪican)

(2) w

    w + a   ɔ (w a s)   (w ɔ s)

(3) l

    a + l   ɔ: (f a l)   (f ɔ :l)

    a + l + lab.   ā/æ

                  (k a l m) (k a:m) but (h ɑ f)

                       beside (h æ f)

    o + l cons.   oᵘ (b o l ə)   (b o u l

(4) r

    a + r   a. (a/r ə)   (a:(r)) are

    ā + r   ɛ (ɛ a:r ə) (: ɛ (r)) care

    o + r   i a: (d o r) (d a.(r)k) dark

               ii ɒ (o r ə)   h ɒr) er

    i + r   ɒ: (b i r d) (ɒ:(r)) d

    ō + r   i ə: (pour)

               ii u: (no r)

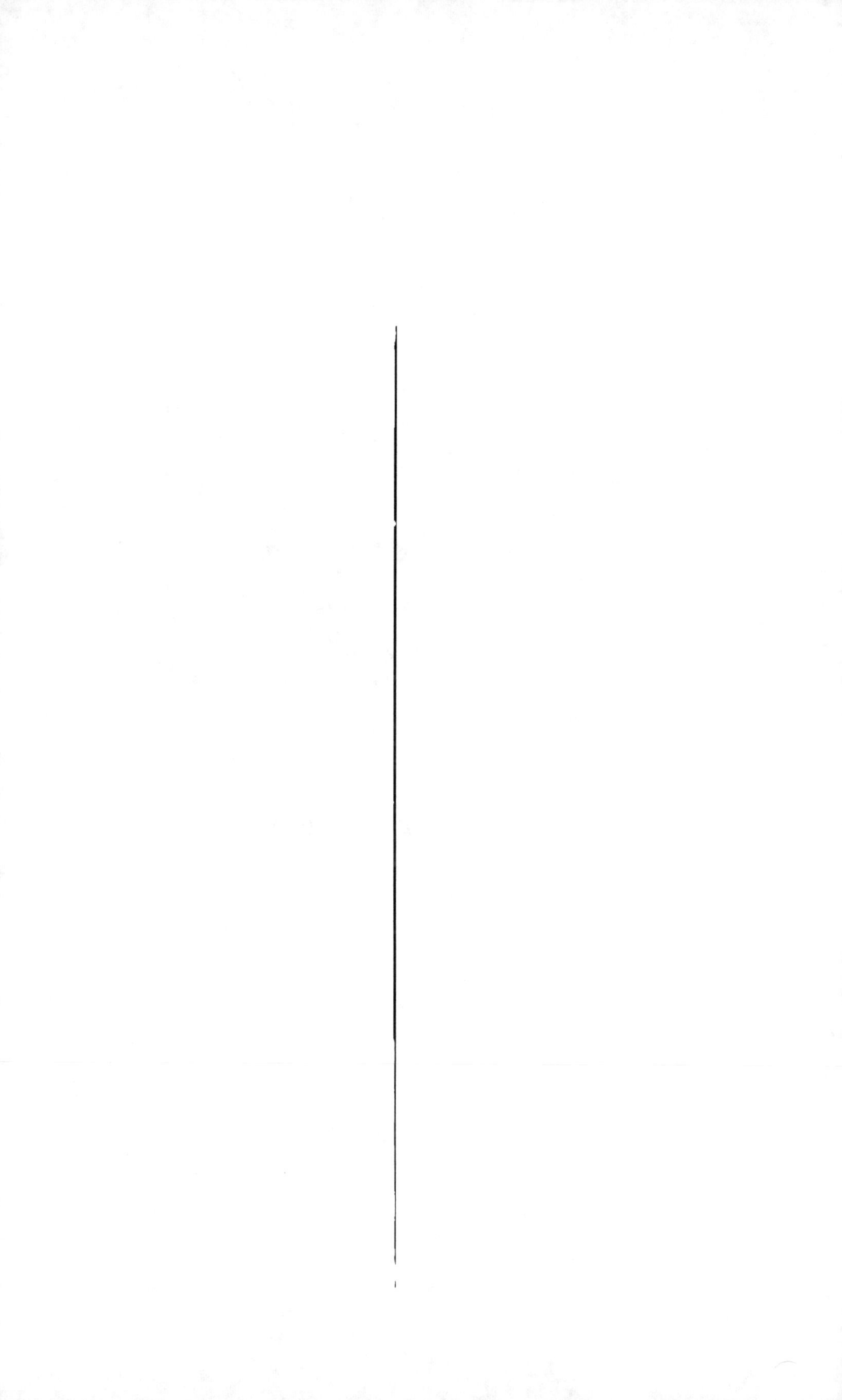

I   II
____

(4)   r   (cont'd)

ō + r   i   ꞔə (ʂ ɘ:ə   r)   ŋ ʝliʃh

             ii   sou ər   near or.

u + r   ʌ: (ʃ ʌ:r)

ū + r   i u: (b u:r n)

             ii ɘ·   (n ɘ:r n)

II

1. __Loss of Consonants__

   (a) Initial , k, w + r.

      ". . gnawe   ". (n ə :)

      " knight ".. (nait)

      " wrest "." . (rest)

   (b) Medial 1 plus m, k, f ; and r + consonant (ngland

      . . palm   ". . (ɡa:m) or (p æ ʃm)

      "." walk   ". . (w ə :k)

      "." half   ". . (h a : f) or (h æ f)

      "." forth   ". . (fə: θ)   (n land)

   (c) Final b after m; ɡ after n, r (n land), gh.

      "... comb ".. (k o: m)

      "... long   . . (l o ŋ)

      "... far ". . (f a :ə)   (n land)

      "... right ".. (r a i t)

2. __Voicing of consonants__

      f, s, ʃ > (v) , (z), (ð) In a stressed wr
                                         syllables.

      ". . of   . . (ə v)

      . . as   ... (æ z)

      ". . with   . . (w i ð)

3. __Final gh so etimes becomes (f).__

   "." rough   ". .   (r u f)

APPENDIX

A CHART OF ORTHOGRAPHIC CHANGES

Note: a blank space means that at that period or in t'
       consideration did not exist.

       Vowels. 10   11   12

       ae sound.   (From O.E. ae and the smoothing

   Nth.   ae/ea
 . Mid.   ae/ea
 . Mid.   ae/ea
   S.   ae/ea
   Kt.   -/ea

       no sound.   (From O.E. ae and the smoothing

   Nth.   ae/ea   ae/ea
 . Mid.   ae/ea   ae/ea
 . Mid.   ae/ea   ae/ea
   S.   ae/ea   ae/ea
   Kt.   ea

       _ sound.   (From O.E. a,O.._.ae, and the sm
   Nth.   a   a/ae/ea   a/ae/ea
 . Mid.   a   a/ae/ea   a/ae/ea
 . Mid.   a   a/ae/ea   a/ae/ea

APPENDIX   III

A Chart of Orthographic Changes in Vowels

Vowels	10	11	12	13	14	15

e. sound. (From O.E. e; ae oa S.W. only; ea, eo in E Mid., Kt.; y in Kt.)

	10	11	12	13	14	15
Nth.	e.	e	e	e	e	e
.Mid.	e.	e	e	e	e	e
E.Mid.	e.	e/oo	e/eo	e	e	e
S.W.	e/ae/ea	e/ae/ea	e/ae/ea	e	e	e
Kt.	e/y	e/eo/ie	e/eo/ie	e	e	e

ę sound. (From O.E. ē; O.E.Y, ae, Io > Ie in Kt.; O.E. eo in Nth., E.Mid., Kt.)

	10	11	12	13	14	15
Nth.	e/eo	e/eo	e/ie	e/ie	ee/(ie)	ie/eo
.Mid.	e	e	e/ie	e/ie	ee/(ie)	ie/ee
E.Mid.	e/oe	e/eo	e/ie	e/ie	ee/(ie)	ie/ee
S. .	e	e	æ/ie	e/ie	ee/ie/ye	ie/eo
Kt.	e/y	e	e/ie/ye	o/ie/ye		ie/eo
			eo/io	eo/io		

ę sound (From O.E. aē,ēa and possibly O.E. ū in Nth.) ey/ai/ay

	10	11	12	13	14	15
Nth.			e/ae/ea	e/ae	e/ea/ei	ea
.Mid.			e/ae/ea	e/ea	e/ea	ea
E.Mid.			e/ae/ea	e/ea	e/ea	ea
S. .			e/ae/ea	e/ea	e/ea	ea
Kt.			e/ae/ea	e/ea	e/ea	ea

i sound. (From O.E. i, O.E. ie in S., O.E. io in Nth., and raising of e to i in Kt.)

	10	11	12	13	14	15
Nth.	i/y/io	i/y	i/y	i/y	i/y	i/y
.Mid.	i/y	i/y	i/y	i/y	i/y	i/y
E.Mid.	i/y	i/y	i/y	i/y	i/y	i/y
S. .	i/y/io	i/y	i/y	i/y	i/y	i/y
Kt.	i/y	i/y	i/y	i/y	i/y	i/y

A P P E N D I X   III   pe

A Chart of Orthgraphic Changes in Vowels

	10	11	12	13	14	15

ī sound. (From O.E. ī, O.L. īo in J.E., O.E. īo final in Kt. becoming īo

	10	11	12	13	14	15
Nth.	i/y	i/y	i/y	i/y	i/y	i/y
. Mid.	i/y	i/y	i/y	i/y	i/y	i/y
. Mid.	i/y	i/y	i/y	i/y	i/y	i/y
S.W.	i/y/ie	i/y	i/y	i/y	i/y	i/y
Kt.	i/y	i/y	i/y/ie	i/y	i/y	i/y

ŏ sound. (From O.E. o, and o/a plus a nasal in W.Mid.)
        His sound is written o in all dialects and periods.

ō sound. (From O.E. ō, and O.L. cons. plus w becoming wō and then wō)

A Chart of Orthographic changes cont'd

	10	11	12	13	14	15
ū sound. (From O... ū or short u when lengthened, and from O.F ǝ), ū̄.						
Nth.	u	u	u	u/o	u/o	u/o
...Mid.	u	u	u	u/o	u/o	u/o
L. 1d.	u	u	u	u/o	u/o	u/o
J..	u	u	u/o	u/o	u/o	u/o
At.	u	u	u/o	u/o	u/o	u/o

ú sound (From O... y, and J... to becomin y)						
..th.	y					
.Mid.	y	y	u	u	u	u
.1d.	y					
J..	y	y	u	u	u	u
it.						

ū̄ sound (From O.. ȳ, .J. fo, and ō in Nth.)						
.th.	y			u/o/ui/uy	u/ui/uy	u/ui/uy
.1d.	y	y	u/ui	u/ui	u/ui	u/ui
.1d.	y					
J..	y	y		u/ui	u/ui	u/ui
it.						

NOTES

Chapter I.

(I) Dates of M.E. period.
"Roughly speaking,fully developed M.E. may be said to extend
from 1150 to 1450".-Sweet,History of English Sounds,p.154.
"The M.E. period(is) bet een roughly,1100 and 1450".-
                    yld,Short History of English,p.81
See also Emerson,A Middle English Reader,Intro.XIII and XIV.

(2) Midland in London dialect.
"Auch in Dialektunterschieden,die sich erst im Mittelengl-
lischen herausbilden,zeigt die Londoner Sprache ein Fort-
schreiten vom Südlichen zum Mittellündischen"-Jordan,Hand-
buch der Mittelenglischen Grammatik,p.28.
"Die Sprache Londons---Im Vierzehnten Jahrhundert zeigen sich
solche Züge in noch weiterem Umfange,so dass die Sprache als
Ganzes einen stark englischen Charakter trägt".-Luick,Hist-
orische Grammatik der Englischen Sprache,p.5
"The London dialect---approximated more closely to the North-
east Midland dialect type at the end of the M.E. period".-
Moore,Historical Outlines,p.113.

(3) The general tendency to give an earlier date to M.E.
sound changes,and to include so-called New English changes in
the M.E. period may be seen from the following quotations:
"The transition period from Old to Middle English is not the
twelfth century as the grammarians used to think,nor even the
eleventh as most of them think now,but rather the tenth".
Kemp Malone,"When Did M.E. Begin?",Curme Volume of Linguistic
                    Studies,Language Monographs,vol.5,p.///
"From the phonology of the early English loan-words in Welsh,
we can safely infer that M.E. ō and ū had passed into (i:)
and (u:) and that M.E. i and u had become fully developed
diphthongs toward the beginning of the fifteenth century.It
is,moreover,certain that M.E. ē in French loan-words---had
passed into (i:)---at least as early as the second half of
the fourteenth century,and we have strong reasons for assum‡
ing that at this date the same sound change occurred in
words of English origin also.---M.L. ī and ū to (u:),(uw) had
already begun in the second half of the fourteenth century"-
R.E.Zachrisson,"The Early English Loan-words in Welsh and the
Chronology of the English Sound Shift",Studies in English
Philology in Honour of Frederick Klaeber,p.306.
See also R.Jordan,Handbuch der Mitteleng. Gr.,pp.230-246.

(4) For some effects of Anglo-Norman script on O.E. script,‡
see G.F.Flom,"Anglo-Norman Script and the Script of Twelfth
Century MSS. in Northeastern Norway",Studies in Eng.Phil. in
Honour of Frederick Klaeber,pp.278-283.

(5) On Scandinavian settlements,see Jordan,Handbuch der
Mittelong.Gr. sec.9.

(6) Analogy: Wyld,A Short History,p.49; yld,Historical Study
of the Mother Tongue,pp.128-141;Jespersen,A Modern English
Grammar,sec. I.7.

Chapter II.

(7) ǣ- O.E. ǣ̸ǣ arose from two sources:
      (i) P.G. ǣ --P.O.L. ǣ--O.E. ǣ
      (ii)P.G. ai plus i/j--P.O.E. ū plus i/j--O.E.ǣ
The two developed differently in O.E. dialects.
    ǣ¹-- Angl. ǭ   ǣ²-- Angl. ǣ
      .S. ǣ   .S. ǣ
      Kt. ē   Kt. ē
It may be seen that Kt. has ē from both sources; .S. has
ǣ from both sources;but there is variation in Angl.
See Luick,Hist. Gr. der Eng. Spr.,'Die Beseitigung des æ
Lautes',pp.341-346;and Jordan,Handbuch der Mittelong, Spr.,
                         pp.71-74.

(8) O.E. developments:E.L.Wardale,An Old English Grammar,
Treatment of the Accented Vowels in the O.E. dialectspp.37-40
also,Wright,An Old English Grammar,Chap.IV.

Chapter III.

(9) Division of syllables,see Wardale,An Old Eng.Grammar,p.12.

(10) Objections to the terms 'palatal' and 'guttural'-Wyld,
A Short History of Eng.,p.38.
"If Palatal means 'formed with the roof of the mouth',then
it may be said that all consonants made by the tongue are
formed between this and some part of the roof of the mouth.-
--.e shall do well to get rid for ever of this unmeaning term".
                         sec.27.
"As a rule the consonants of European languages are formed in
the mouth.This being so it is better to discard altogether the
misleading term guttural".-sec.24

(11) Symbol: long æ- Scholars disagree as to whether there
was a sound change in the passage of O.E. ǣ to M.E. long,
open e. right says the change was merely orthographical,but
Wyld,Moore and Jespersen say that there was a development in
sound. Wyld and Moore would describe the change as a shifting
from a front unround lax vowel (æ) to a front unround tense

vowel (ɛ:).Since ˉyld says that the long æ is tho same as ɔ
short æ longthened,I havo used the æ symbol to oxpress tho
long vowel phonetically.

(I2) (∅) These sounds have dropped out of English, and in
M.E. they were expressed in a number of ways,so that it is
difficult to namo them other then in phonotic symbols.Both
Wyld and Jespersen oxpress the first two sounds by the ∅,∅:
symbols,although Moore uses the œ ,œ : symbols for them.

Chaptor IV.

(I3) Anglo-Norman influence on orthography:
Emerson,A ME. Reader,Intro.,pp.XVIII and XIX.
Jordan,Handbuch der Littolong. Gr.,sec. I7.
Moore,Historical Outlines,sec. I20.
Luick,Hist. Gr. der Eng. Spracho,sec. 57.
Wyld,Short History,p.83.

(I4) æ- A.Pogatscher,"Dio Lnglische æ/e Grenze"(Anglia XXIII
p.206-)shows tho developments,their spellings,and their dialectal regions from placo-names.Endorsed by Miss Serjeantson
in "Dovelopment of O.E. eag/eah in M.E.".

(I5) ca spolling- Jordan,sec.I8,p.35

(I6) o spelling- Moore,Historical outlinos,sec. I20.

(I7) Spelling of o for u- Jordan,sec. I7; Luick,Hist.Gr.sec.57.2

(I8) Spolling of ou for u- Jordan,I7.I.
(I9)
(I9) u symbol for y,-Luick,sec.57.I; Jordan,I7.I.

(20) M.E. spollings for O.E. c- Jordan,I7.2.

(2I) O.L. g- Wardalo,An O.L. Grammar,secs.4.c and 72;
                                        Jordan,I6.

(22) Spellings for h- Jordan,I7.2.

(23) þ and ð -.right,An Elementary M.E. Grammar,&sec.20

(24) sc- Jordan,sec.I8I,"Im M.E. ontstand otwa um II00 aus
sx nit Verschmolzung beide hauto s, worauf dio Französischon
Shroibungen s,so deuten".

n im Frühaltenglischen bestand eine Tendenz zur Beseit-
 überlanger Silbenquantität durch Kürzung langer Vokale
ehrfacher Konsonanz;so vom 7 Jahrh. ab vor drei Konson-
.Gegen Ende der ao..eit,im I0 Jahrh. und namentlich in
ahrzehnten um I000 werden Vokale und Diphthonge auch vor
Konsonanten und vor längen Konsonanten gekürzt".
                        Jordan,Handbuch,sec. 23.
chfalls noch vor II00 wurden lange Vokale vor einfachen
nanten-auch vor sonst dehnenden Konsonantengruppen-in
ilbigen orten gekürzt".Jordan,Handbuch,sec.24.
k notes a further dialectal shortening:
einlich früher Zeit,jedenfalls vor dem I3 Jahrh.,und
inem Gebiet,das hauptsächlich das westliche Mittelland,
auch einige Striche des Nordens umfasste,scheint u in
er Silbe vor gutturalen und labialen Dauerlauten,also
,v,m verkürst worden zu sein".Hist.Gr.,sec.389.
shortening of long vowels in trisyllabic words began
o the change of (a:) to (ə:)".-Moore,Hist.Outlines,
                        sec.27.I (a).
lso Luick,Hist. Gr.,secs. 352-354; Wyld,Short History,
I75-I77; Jesperson, . Modern Grammar,secs.4.3I-4.4.

Variations due to shortening:
owel variations in related forms due to shortening should
ted particularly in connection with (I)sc and st.Short-
 took place in the nominative of words ending thus,but
n the inflected cases.For instance,O.L. ȳäst should give
gast,and the shortened form does survive in N.E.ghastly,
he vowel of the noun ghost comes from the inflected cases-
s-of the O.E. noun,in which shortening did not occur.On
ther hand,the shortened form of the nominative survived
ch words as dust,fist,wish from O.E. dūst,fȳst,wȳsc.
e preterites and past participles of verbs.The variation
wel length between the infinitive nd the past tenses is
 the result of shortening -O.E. fēdau gives M.E. feden
.E. feed;while the preterite O.L. fĕdde gives M.L. fedde
.E. fed.The same is true of N.E. lead(infin.) beside led.
o comparison of adjectives.In the comparative form,shor-
e should occur before the consonant group-O.L. dēoppra
d become M.E. depper,but this form has disappeared in
 of one with the long vowel from the nominative.Thus,
dēop gives N.E. deep,and this vowel is carried into the
comparative form deeper.(4) Abstract nouns with suffix.
ifference in vowel values between N.E. nouns and adjec-
 and their derivatives is due to shortening.O.L. þēof,
fūl,wīd give N.E.thief,broad,foul,wide;but O.E.þēofþu,
,brædþu,wīdþu,give N.E.theft,filth,broadth and width.
oore.Hist.Outlines.p.94;.vld.Short Hist..sec.I75-I76.n.

(27) Lengthening.
There was an earlier lengthening in L.O.E.,although the conditions were different.The O.E. lengthening of a short vowel
or diphthong occurred before certain consonant groups consisting of either a liquid or a nasal consonant together with
another voiced consonant-nd,mb,ng,ld,rd,rl,rn and probably
rʒ,rs.This lengthening occurred probably as early as the 9th
century.However,in the transitional period between O.E. and
M.E.,the vowels which had lengthened before the r plus consonant groups shortened again;and later,during the M.E. period
those before nd,ng shortened.Nevertheless,there are many cases
in which this lengthened vowel survives the M.E. shortening,
although apparently only before the ld,mb combinations to any
extent.Hence the long vowel in N.E. child,comb.
    On the O.E. lengthening,see Jordan,Handbuch,sec.22;Wyld,Short
History,sec.II4;and Jespersen,A Modern Grammar,sec.4.22I,
although Jesperson says that "some,not all vowels" were affected by this lengthening.

    On the M.E. lengthening,Moore notes"In the thirteenth century
the short vowels,a,e,and o were lengthened in open syllables
of dissyllabic words"-Hist.Outlines,sec.27(b).
"It is now pretty generally accepted that,as stated by Luick,
i and u in open syllables were lengthened,lowered and made
tense,before the beginning of the fourteenth century"-Wyld,
                    Short History,sec.I74.
See also Jespersen,A Modern Eng. Gr.,secs.4.2II-4.223.

    Jespersen,in discussing the general problem of quantitative
changes,disagrees with the application of a theory advanced
by Luick(Anglia XX,335ff.) which Jespersen summarized as "a
general tendency to reduce the length of stressed syllables
to a normal measure,namely in words of <u>one</u> syllable a short
vowel plus a long consonant(or two consonants) or a long
vowel and a short consonant;in words of <u>two</u> syllables a short
vowel plus a short consonant or a long vowel without any consonant;and in words of <u>three</u> syllables a short vowel without
a consonant."-Mod.Eng.Gr.,sec.4.I2.

<u>Chapter VI</u>.

(28) The phonetic symbols have been given only where confusion might arise.Otherwise,where the written symbol and the
phonetic symbol agree,the phonetic symbol has not been given.

(29) a/o plus nasal.
Moore,Hist. Outlines,sec.69.2,notes the ..Mid. o plus nasal
as distinguishing that dialect from E.Mid. .yld,Short

History,sec.161 says"In the W.Mid. we find _an_ in the s outhern
portion of the area,but _on_ as the characteristic type in the
Central and Morthern parts of the area".
Mackenzie,Early London Dialect,p.132, observes"While O.E. a
plus nasal generally appears in M.L. texts of the S.E. and
S.E.Mid. area as _an_,there are traces of _on_ forms.However,
genuine _on_ forms do not seem to occur in London documents at
any time during the M.L. period".

(30) e --i plus nch.
e became i "vor gedeckten Nasal,namentlich im Norden und an-
grenzeden Teilen des Mittellandes,aber auch wie es scheint in
einem Teil des Südens"-Luick,Hist.Gr.,sec.379.
Also see Jespersen,Mod.Eng.Gr.,sec.3.113.

(31) Æ-See note (7),Chapter II.

(32) ȝ
"In the North and in the E.Midlands---O.E. y is unrounded
probably in the late O.E. period.M.L. texts from these areas
write i or y for the original (y) sound.
"In the O.E. period,O.E. y had become e in Kent and Suffolk.
In S.E. and S.E.Midland texts of the M.L. period these sounds
continue and are written in the old way.
"In by far the greater part of England,that is to say in the
whole of the W.Mid. and Central Mid.,---O.E. y remains with,
approximately,its original sound,at any rate well into the
fifteenth centruy".-Wyld,Short History,secs.,158 (a),(b),(c).
   In his article on "The Treatment of O.E. y in Dialects of
Mid. and South-Eastern Counties in M.L."(Englische Studien,
vol.47,pp 45-46),Wyld subdivides these districts into u,i
and e areas.
See also Jordan,Handbuch,secs.39-44.

(33)Northern dialect.
See Morsbach,Mitteleng.Gr.,sec.6;Wyld,Short History,sec.206,
summary of Nth.;Luick,Hist.Gr.,sec.406,"Die nordhumbrische
Umbildung des o-Lautes".

(34) Nth ā--(ɛ:)
Wyld,Short Hist.,sec.157,"As regards the sound,this must have
been advanced,and fronted to (æ:) pretty early,and this was
subsequently raised to (ɛ:) and (e:).--It is impossible to
say with anything like certainty when the fronting process
began".

(35) On the E.Mid. dialect,see Wyld,Short History,sec. 205 for
a comparative table of the Midland dialects;also Moore,Histori-
cal Outlines,secs.68,69; Morsbach,Mitteleng. Gr.,sec;7; Morris,
Introduction to Genesis and Exodus,E.E.T.S.

(36)The W.Mid. dialect.
Serjeantson,"Dialects of the W.Midland",Review of Eng.Studies,
vol. 3,gives a summary of Morsbach,Jordan,Wyld,Luick and Menner
on the distinction between W.Mid. and E.Mid..She then examines
eight texts for W.Mid. characteristics,and finally,from this ex
-amination differentiates North,Central and South W.Mid.
Menner,"Four Notes on the W.Midland Dialect", I.L.H.,vol.41,com-
ments on W.Mid. final i/y:"The extent to which final i/y is still
written e in the W.Mid. of late fourteenth and early fifteenth
centuries has not been recognised",p.455. "This sound change
would correspond phonetically to the process by which W.Mid.un-
stressed e before single final consonants tended to become a
lower vowel expressed in spelling by u",p.457.
See also Wyld,sec.205;Moore,secs.68,69.

(37) On the S.W. dialect see the following summaries:Moore,sec.
66;Wyld,sec.204;Jordan,sec.4;Morsbach,sec. 9.a.

(38) On the Kt. dialect see summaries in Wyld,sec.203;Moore,sec
67;and Heuser,"Zum Kent. Dialekt im Mittelenglische",Anglia,vol
17,pp.75-90.

<u>Chapter VIII</u>

(39) O.E. diphthongic symbols in M.E.
Jordan,sec.18, "Nachdem ae. ea beim Übergang zum Me. zu æ--e
monophthongiert war,war ea als traditionelle Schreibung zunächst
beibehalten und auch für die Fortsetzung des ae. ea verwandt
worden".

(40) ēa
Mackenzie,"A Special Dialectal Development of O.E. ēa in M.E."
Englische Studien,vol.61,"In certain M.E. texts,the vowel from
O.E. ēa rimes systematically --with undoubted M.E. (o:) from
O.E. ō/ōo",p.586. The dialect character of these texts is S.
Eastern or S.E.Mid.,p.578.
Serjeantson,"The Development of O.E. ēag/ēah in M.E.",Journal
of Eng. and Germ. Phil.,vol.26,pp.800-803,gives a summary of
the development.
    By the end of the O.E. period,ō h/ēag had become ōh/ēg,and
then became . . ōh/ēg.
                O.E: ēag(e)--ēg(e)--oig(e) -----------oi(e)
                                                       ī(e)
                                                       īh
                            oih   ----------oih
                   ēah   --ōh -----------------------ōh
The e type appears most frequently in South East
The ch "   "   "   "   "   "   "   East
The oi "   "   "   "   "   "   Midland

Menner,"Four Notes on the W.Midland Dialect",M.L.R.,vol.41,
p.454,notes a W.Mid. spelling o from O.E. ēa forms as in the
word 'yord'.He suggests that this indicates a shifting of stress
to the second element of the ēa diphthong before ā became ō.
On ea diphthong see Jordan,secs.56-64,81-83;Wyld,secs.164-167

(41) eo

Jordan,secs. 65-73,84-76;Wyld,secs. 168,169.

(42) io
Jordan,secs. 74,84-86; Wyld,sec.170.

(43) Kentish diphthongs.
Wyld,sec. 166,"It seems possible that in Kt. the O.E. diphthongs survived in some forms as diphthongs into the M.E. per
-iod,O.E.ea probably becoming a 'rising diphthong'.
However,Taylor,"On the History of O.E. ēa/ēo in Middle Kent."
M.L.R.,vol.19,pp.1-10,opposes the theory of the Kt. rising
diphthong.He makes two points:
(i)"There is no strong evidence against the assumption of a
development in Kt. of these diphthongs parallel to that of
other dialects in general",p.2.
(ii)"The fact that all the variant forms representing O.E. ēa
are found already in the twelfth century (Prose Genesis)makes
it possible to assume that such spellings in the fourteenth
century may be merely archaic forms-traditional spellings for
a sound which had existed in the twelfth century or earlier,
but was by the fourteenth century entirely lost",p.8.

Chapter VIII.

(44) M.E.(bou) from M.E. bough is a development from the inflected cases of O.E. bōh,and hence the gh does not become f-
see Jespersen, Modern Eng. Gr.,sec. 10.25.
The development of th diphthong falls in with the change from
M.E. ū. Wyld,sec.246,says of the ū,"The series of changes from
the old long vowel to the (modern) diphthong was probably
(u--uᵘ--ou--au)!Hence,M.E. bough has the same vowel sound as
the verb,bow,from O.E. būgan.

(45) The development of new diphthongs.
Luick,Hist. Gr.,sec.573 An m I,"Die Frühesten zeugnisse für
diesen Wandel sind nicht Schreibungen——in Hss. des 12 Jahr-
hunderts,die nur Velslisierung des serweisen,wohl aber der
Reim lele (ao.log)——und die Schreibungen bei Orm".

(46) O.E. flōogan,lōogan in M.E.
The modern form of these words comes from the M.E. Mid.
Moore,sec. 27.5.b,"An Old English ō followed by the (j) sound
that developed in Middle English out of Old English ( ) be-
came Middle English (ei) which developed later into Middle
English (i:);e.g. Mercian O.E. lēgan (W.S.lēogan),M.E. leie(n)
(leiən),later lie(n) (li:ən)".
See also Jordan,sec. 98.

(47) Periods of development.
Moore,p.27,"The special developments resulting in new diphthongs and in (i:) and (u:) did not all occur at the same per
-iod.The earliest to occur were those that resulted in the com
bination of vowels with Old English w and with the (j) sound
that was already (j) in Old English;and the next were those
that resulted from the combination of vowels with h".
See also Jordan,secs. 88-IOI,III-I29.

(48) Back ȝ in Kt.
Jordan,sec. III"Der stimhaft guttural Spirant ȝ wurde in In-
laut von I200 ab zu w (u) vokalisiert ʒ̯ (zuerst in S.W.L.,
erst gegen I400 in Kent)". He gives as examples mage,lage.

(49) Early Vocalising of w in O.E.
Jordan,sec. 87," uch bildete silbenauslautendes w Diphthonge
mit vorhergehenden Langen,z.Beow. snaw̯ snau,stow̯=stou".
See also below,sec. 28.I,hreouw.

(50) Diphthongs with w.
See Moore,p.26 on the sources of the (au) and (ə:u) diphthongs;Jordan,sec.87,I04-IIO.

(5I) Diphthongs with f.
Wyld,sec.I7I.4," W.E. eu- O.E. and M.E. ef plus consonant becomes ew in Late M.E.". Sec.I7I.7.b,"af-followed by a vowel
becomes av,aw."
See also Jespersen,sec.2.555.

(52) Diphthongs with nas als.
Wyld,s ec.I7I.9 (note),"The O.E. combination -enct becomes
eint,chiefly in S.W.".
Jordan,sec.I03,"Verwandt ist die Entstehung von ei aus e vor
den palatalen Gruppen nct,ngd,ng ,wobei sich eint,eind,ein
ergeben"--cites examples from Mid.,S.W. and Kt. texts.

(53) Diphthongs with sh/nsh.
Wyld,sec. I7I.9 (note),"The combinations (a ʃ ,antʃ,and z)in
some dialects (Sth.-Western?) often become diphthongal in M.E."

Jordan,sec.I02,"Fast auf dem ganzen Gebiet,doch mit Tendenz
zu s pateren Vorwiegen im Westen ergab sich zwischen a,e und
e ein Ubergangs laut i,soø dass die Gruppen ais,eis entstand
-en".

<u>Chapter IX.</u>

(54) Vocalising of ʒ/w.
See Wright,Elementary M.E. Gr.,secs.240,24I;Jordan,secs.I55,
I56.

(55) Unvoicing of g,d finally,see Wright,secs.258,259;Jordan,
sec.I95,"So erhielt sich dann auch die Verhartung zu nk---
nun auch in betonter Silbe hauptsächlich in MIL";sec.200,
"Im Mittelland ist durchgehendes þ in unbetonter Silbe ein
kriterium des Westens;in Nordenglischen begegnet es nur unter
beschränkten Bedingungen (namentlich wieder nach r,l)".

(56) Disappearance of consonants,see Moore,sec.50.I;Wright,
sec. 250.

(57) listen.
The N.E.D. gives O.N. lysna as the source of M.E. listen,and
notes the O.E. cognate hlosnian.On the t it says,"The forms ½
with t are due to association with the synonymous <u>list</u>."

(58) Voicing of f,ƒ,s,see Moore,sec. 66.2;Wright,sec.256;'yld
secs.202.6-7,204.6.

(59) s e,see Jordan,s ecs. I8I-I85;Wright,sec.289.

(60) dusk.
The N.E.D. gives the following note,"The relation of modern
dusk to O.E. dox,presents some difficulties both as to the
vowel and to the final consonant group.Few of our words in sk
are of O.E. origin".The M.E. forms deosc,dosc,deosk,dosk,dusko
dusk,are cited.

(6I) c see Kaluza,secs.265,267;Jordan,secs.I78-I80;Wright,ƒƒ
secs.280-288.

(62) g see Wright,secs. 290-299;Jordan,secs. I84ø -I94.

(63) Final h becoming f.
Jordan,sec.I96 An m; Wright,sec.899.

(64) Nth. hw--hw,see Jordan,sec.I95; Wright,sec.303.

Chapter X.

(65) Weakening of unstressed vowels.
Moore,sec. 29.I.I;Jordan,sec.I34-I4I.

(66) Date of weakening.
Moore,sec. 29.I.I,"This development was completed by the year
II00 in the Southern dialect,at least as early or earlier in
the Midland dialect,and perhaps as early as the year I000 in
the Northern dialect".

(67) Dialectal differences in inflections.
Vowels- Jordan,sec. I55,"In Norden ging es in i über,wahrend
es in Mittelland zwischen i und e verharrte.In westlichen Mit
-telland aber entstand ein dunklerer Laut,der in der Schreibung mit u wiedergegeben wird".
Loss of final n.
Moore,"Loss of Final n in Inflectional Syllables",Language,
vol.IV,p.252, "In no respect,perhaps,do the Southern and Midland M.E. texts show greater differences the n in the loss or
retention of/ the final n of unstressed inflectional syllables
   "In"The Owl and the Nightingale",we find an approximation
to the complete loss of final n in all the unstressed inflectional syllables that developed from the O.E. endings -an,-un
-on,and -en"
   In the London English of Chaucer there is complete loss of
final n in the singular of weak nouns.There is also complete
loss of the nasal in both the strong and weak adjective inflections,except for the survival of the O.E. ending -an or
-un in -self compounds such as myselven etc."

Chapter XI.

(68) Levelling in nouns,see Moore's summary of the analogical
changes in the inflections of nouns,sec.46(Hist.Outlines);
Wyld,secs.3I3,3I5.

(69) Weak declensions in S.W. and Kt.
Wyld,sec. 3I3,"In M.E. this form (weak) of declension is largely extended in the Sthn. and Kentish texts,so that many originally strong words are included".

(70) Adjective endings.
Wyld,sec. 324,"The declension of adjectives u dergoes considerable modifications in M.E. b the natural process of levelling all the vowels of the endings under -e"

(71) Weak declension;see Moore,sec.50;Wyld sec.325.

(72) Strong declension,see Moore,sec.49; yld,sec.325.

Chapter XII.

(73) The definite article.
Wyld,sec.389,"For the Nom. Sing. se,seo,a form þo is substituted which owes its þ to the analogy of the initial in
the forms of all the other cases,Sing. and Pl. This indeclinable form is found to some extent,even in the South,in
the earliest texts,alongside of the inflected forms".
Menner,"Four Notes on the Midland Dialect",M.L.R.,vol.41,
p.457,comments on the form þo-"The form may be considered
characteristic of the Northwestern and perhaps Central Mid-
lands,though it would be rash to say that it is never found
in the East".

(74) The demonstrative pronouns,see Moore,sec. 55;Wyld,sec.
395.

(75) I from ich,see above,the disappearance of consonants,
sec.53.3.

(76) us from us,see above,shortening in unstressed words,
sec.13.4.

(77) ʒu/ʒou/ʒuw/ you forms.
Moore,sec.53,"One explanation regards the ʒ-forms as analogy
formations developed from the (:u) forms under the influence
of the nominative ʒe,with later change of (:u) into (u:).A
simpler explanation is that they developed from the Middle
English (iu) forms as the result of the falling diphthong becoming a rising diphthong".

(78) Third person plural.
Wyld,sec.307,"The point of interest in the Pl. forms is the
gradual introduction and substitution for the native forms of
the forms þei,þaim,þeir,and their variants,which are of Scandinavian origin.71 It would appear that few pure Southern or
Kentish texts have any of these forms before the fifteenth
century".
Menner,"Four Notes on the Midland Dialect",M.L.R.vol.41,
p.458,remarks on her(t eir)."The use of her as the possessive
plural pronoun is well recognised as a characteristic of the
W.Mid. or Southwestern dialects.It is perhaps worth noting
that it persists in the W.Mid. later than in the Southwest".

Another strange form in M.E. pronouns is the feminine she.
Harald Lindkvist,"On the History and Origin of the English Pro
-noun 'she',Anglia,vol.45,says,"On no account are we justified
in considering the O.E. demonstrative seo s the source of the
M.E. s ho,she in the Northern and Midland dialects",p.IO.
We seem justified in presuming th t in Old Northumbrian and
at least the eastern portion of the Mercian dialect,hio passed
into (hjo) or (jo) in the course of the IIth century.At about
the same time the Old Mercian heo became ho in the West and
ho in the East of the Midlands.Owing to the blending of ho
and ʒho,ʒo,there a rose the secondary ʒe.--- s soon as the i
in hio began to be consonantized,the fin l -s of the preceding
verb was gradually shifted on to the pronoun,so that the new
form scho was probably in existence about the year IIOO.In
the North-East Midland dialect another blending took place,this
time/ of scho and the before-mentioned ho or ʒo.The result was
scho(she),of which the earliest recorded instance dates from
the year II40",p.49-50.

<u>Chapter XIII.</u>

(79) O.E. strong verbs and their M.E. equivalents,see Moore,
s ces.57-60;Wyld,secs.343-349.

(80) The Western preterite.
Wyld discusses this peculiarity in sec. 556,where he says that
the preterite is levelled under the type of the Past Part.
However,Andrew,"The Preterite in the North Western Dialects,
Rev. Eng. Studies,vol.5,objects to Wyld's theory and says,"All
the evidence seems to prove quite conclusively that while the
o preterite was the rule in N.E. Northumbrian dialects for cer
-tain classes of verbs(in which there was no good historical)
there was a tendency to extend it by analogy to verbs in which
there was no good historical ground for it;so far as I have ob
-served,it is n t found on this large scale in any but Northumbrian texts,and may therefore be accepted as an additional
test of dialect for that region',p.455.
(This o comes from the preterite of classes IV and V,where the
singular and plural are alike.)
        vowel
(81) O.E. verbs and their M.E. equivalents,see Moore,secs.IIO-
II2;Wyld,secs.538-542.

(82) Dialectal variations in verbal inflections,se th summaries of dialects in Moore and Wyld.

(83) Pret.Pres. verbs,Moore,sec. II7;Wyld,sec.556.

(84) Be,will,do,go, see Moore,sec. 65.

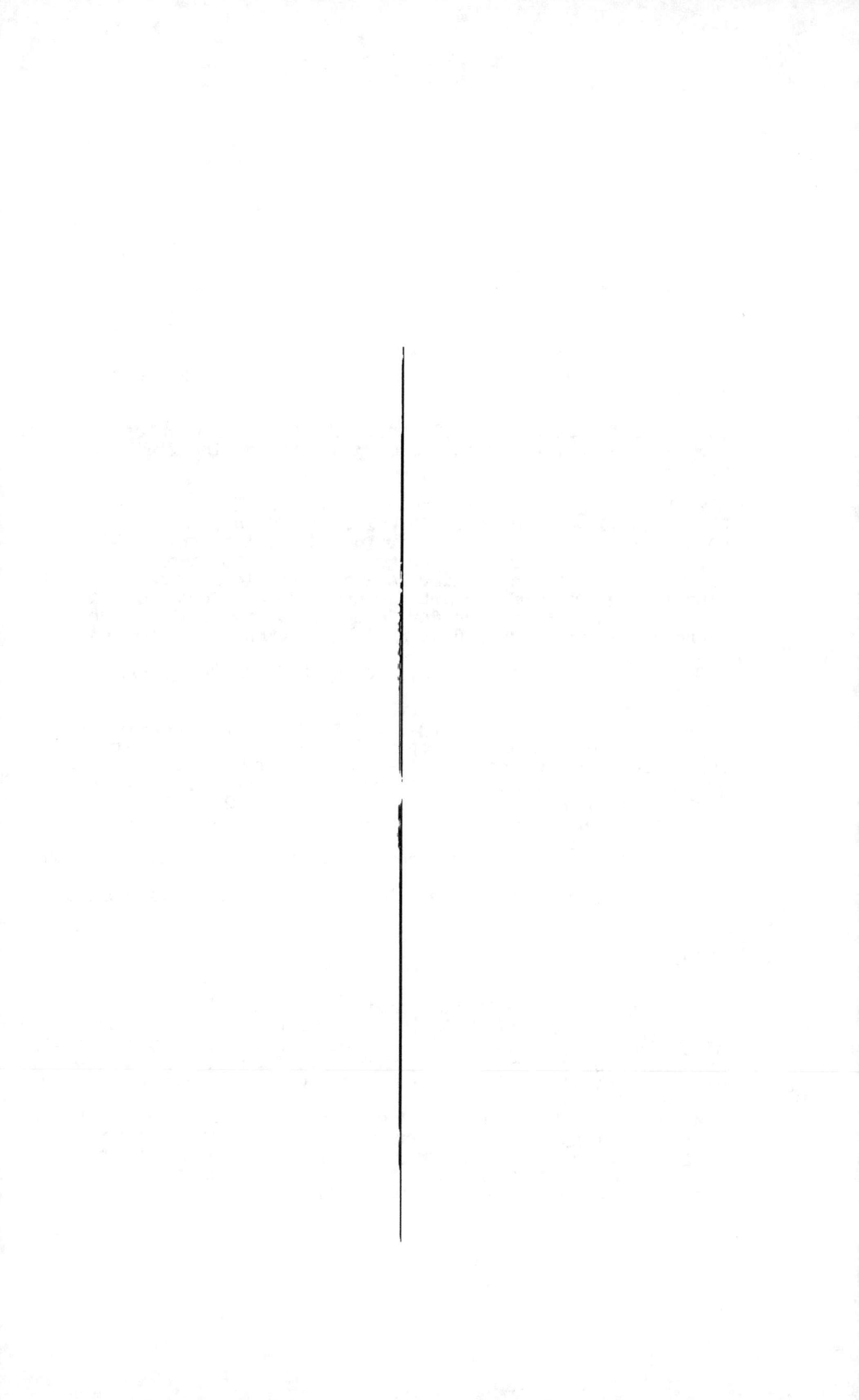

Chapter XIV.

(85) Word order.
Classen,Hist.of the Eng. Lang.,p.55,"One of the most marked features of the transition from O.E. to M.E. syntax is the gradual fixing of the word order".

(86) Article-Huchon,p.205;Classen,p.59,"Another development which occurred in M.E. ---is the development of the indefinite article".

(87) Loss of grammatical gender,see Bradley,The Making of English,pp.47-49;Classen,p.58;Wyld,sec.515; also Moore, "Grammatical and Natural Gender in M.E.",".L.A.,vol.XXXVI, no. I . Moore notes that the general explanation of the introduction of natural gender is due to the loss of gender distinguishing forms of the article and strong adjective.He,however,says that natural gender "came in by way of the personal pronouns" in which such distinguishing forms were retained.

(88) Prepositions,see Laluza,secs.547,548;Classen,p.56.

(89) Impersonal 'it' construction.
Huchon,Hist.de la Langue Ang.,says that the retention of the impersonal constuction is due to French influence."La Tournure Impersonelle,venant de l'Anglo-saxon et confirmé par le fran-çais,se sort du pronom neutro como sujet logique du verbe",p. p.205. Later,he notes 'it' as one of the results of French in-fluence,p.255.

(90) On old interrogatives becoming relatives,see Classen,p.58

(91) Comparison of adjectives by more and most,see Huchon,p.215.

Chapter XV.

(93) Scandinavian influence on inflections.
Bradley,The Making of English,p.31,"There must have arisen mixed dialects,mainly English,but containing many Danish words, and characterised by the dropping or confused use of some of the terminations distinctive of cases,genders and persons".

(94) They and their,see note 78;Classen,p.64; and Emerson,Hist. of the Eng.Language,p.154,when he says,"So powerful was the Danish influence that not only nouns,adjectives and verbs were borrowed,but even pronominal forms as they,their,possibly them, which are Norse rather than English".

(95) Scandinavian sk words;see Emerson,Hist.of the Eng. Lang.,
p. 156;Wright,Elementary M.E. Gr.,sec.161.

(96) Scandinavian suffixes,see Classen,p.65;Emerson,p.154;and on
the whole Scandinavian element,see Wright,pp.80-89.

(97) French element,see Wright,pp.89-106,and on the dates to which
that influence extended,see Wright,sec.182.

(98) French influence on orthography,see above chapter IV.

(99) French influence on syntax,see above,notes 86,89,91.

(100) French influence on vocabulary.
Emerson,Hist.of the Eng.Lang.,p.162,"In all M.E. writings before
1250,the number of French words probably does not exceed 500.By
the year 1500,some 1000 French words were used in written monu-
ments;while in some thirty-one texts written before 1400,Skeat
has discovered 3400 words of French origin".
Classen,p.69,ff.,"When we turn to examine the various classes of
loan words from the French we are able to see in how many differ
-ent ways French civilisation and French culture influenced the
English".He groups the borrowings under titles for governing
officials,war and military terms,fashions,foods,arts,science.
See also Bradley,The Making of Eng.,pp.84-95.

(101) Celtic borrowings,see Emerson,180;Bradley,pp.94-96.

(102) Latin borrowings.
Classen,p.62,"Perhaps as far as M.E. is concerned,special mention
should be made of the Latin translation of the Scriptures---since
many Latin words entering English during the middle period may be
traced to this source".
See also,Sweet,Principles of Eng. Etym.,secs.175-188; Emerson,
Hist.of the Eng.Lang.,p.

(103) Low Country borrowings;see LLewellyn,"The Influence of Low
Dutch on the English Vocabulary",Pub.Phil.Soc.,especially pp.45-
47,where he cites terms brought into English through trade between
Britain and the Low Dutch countries;also,Bradley,The Making of Eng
-lish,p.102;Classen,p.89;Emerson,p.170-172.

<u>Chapter XVI.</u>

(104) Chaucer's dialect.
Lounsbury,Studies in Chaucer,p.453,"He wrote in the East-Midland
dialect.It was largely because he wrote in it that the East-Midland dialect became the language of English Literature".See also,
ten Brink,The Language and Metre of Chaucer,Intro.,xxxi.

(105) ǭ/ǫ from O.F. ōē in Chaucer.
Ten Brink,p.17,p.257. However,see Victor Langhans,"Der Reimvokal ō bei Chaucer",Anglia,vol.45,"Die Theorie,die ten Brink
zur Erklärung der e-Reime bei Chaucer und damit für die Reim-
technik des Dichters überhaupt aufstellte,ist unhaltbar",p.256
"Ein Fehler,der ten Brink Anschauungen zu Grunde liegt,ist
die Annahme,dass Chaucer nur reine,etymologisch genaue Reime
gebaut haben könne und dass man nur ganz vereinzelte Ausnah-
men zugestehen dürfe",p.256.
"Die Qualität des ō wird in der Regel beachtet.----Öfter bei
ǫ von ō von ai-i,besonders aber bei ǫ von ōē von ā in den
der Dichter sich der überkamen literarischen Tradition anbe-
quemt,in welcher der ostmittelländische Einfluss von Ausdruck
kommt",p.592.
Jespersen,A Modern Eng.Gr.,p.sec.I.52,"Chaucer's rimes are as
a rule very correct indeed"—"He does not rhyme ǭ/ǫ".

(106) Breaking.
Wyld,sec.165,"The London Area undoubtedly had fracture origin
-ally before 1 plus consonant.--Chaucer has a few examples---
of the old City and Middlesex type-helde,bihelde.These may
well be due to Chaucer's early connexion with the City".
See also,ten Brink,Language and Metre of Chaucer,p.58.

(107) O.E. lengthening.
Ten Brink,p.11,says that Chaucer has long vowels where there
were "originally short vowels as a rule before ld;original i,
u,y,before nd;i and occasionally a,o,before mb".

(108) a/o plus nasal.
ten Brink,p.38,"O.E. a,o before resonants becomes o before nd
or ng;ō before mb;otherwise a".
Wyld,sec.161.1,"None of the later London texts and documents
have any trace of -on-,nor have the Place Names,neither here
nor in the Eastern counties".

(109) woman,see above,sec.18.5.

(110) ā --ǭ/ǫ.
ten Brink,p.22,"" fluctuation between ǭ and ǫ is shown in
some words,the root vowel of which resulting from O.E. ā was
or is,preceded by w".

(111) y
Wyld,sec.150,(e),"The op forms which occur in the later literary and standard spoken dialect may be regarded as survivals
of the City type,which was virtually identical with the Essex
dialect.Thus,in this respect Chaucer,to judge by his rhymes,
distinctly favours the City type";
ten Brink,p.40,"In Chaucer u o curs only in burden,-bury,and
otherwise exceptionally for the sake of rime.The correct form
in the thesis dialect is e and i.----e in on the whole more fre

(1 2) oo--o/o
ten Brink,p.44,"In the district where Chaucer's language pre-
vails an o develops,but only before w".

(II3) ei--ai written ei,see ten Brink,p.51

(II4) Consonants,see above Chapter IX.

(II5) Northern retention of l and v,see above,sec.52.4.

(II6) Lt.influence in the voicing of f to v,see above,note 58.

(II7) se ,see above sec.53.2.

(II8) c ,see above sec.53.3.

(II9) g ,see above sec.53.4.

(I20) h ,see above sec.53.5.

(I2I) Final (ǝ) see Moore,secs.89-92.

(I22) S./. declension in n uns and adjectives,see above sec.40

(I23) Chaucer's verb forms,see Moore,secs.84-88.

(I24) Chaucer's orthography,see Moore,sec.76.

(I25) Chaucer's vocabulary,see Emerson,p.162,"In Chaucer's
prologue to the Canterbury Tales,the foreign element,mostly
French,is twelve or thirteen percent".

(I26) e͡er --ar,see Jordan,sec.

Chapter XVII .

(I27) Chaucer and Gower,ten Brink,intro.,p.XXX; Luick,Hist.Gr.
sec. 5 .

(I28) ao
Wyld,Sec.I20 (?),"In the London area we find two quite different
types in the early M.E.period,the Eastern or City type which
agrees with that of Essex,and the more central and westerly
dialect which originally had e.----In the fourteenth century
there appear to be no e-spellings in any London or Middlesex
document;the Eastern or City type has won the day'.
See also,Mackenzie, Early London Dialect,sec.24-37.

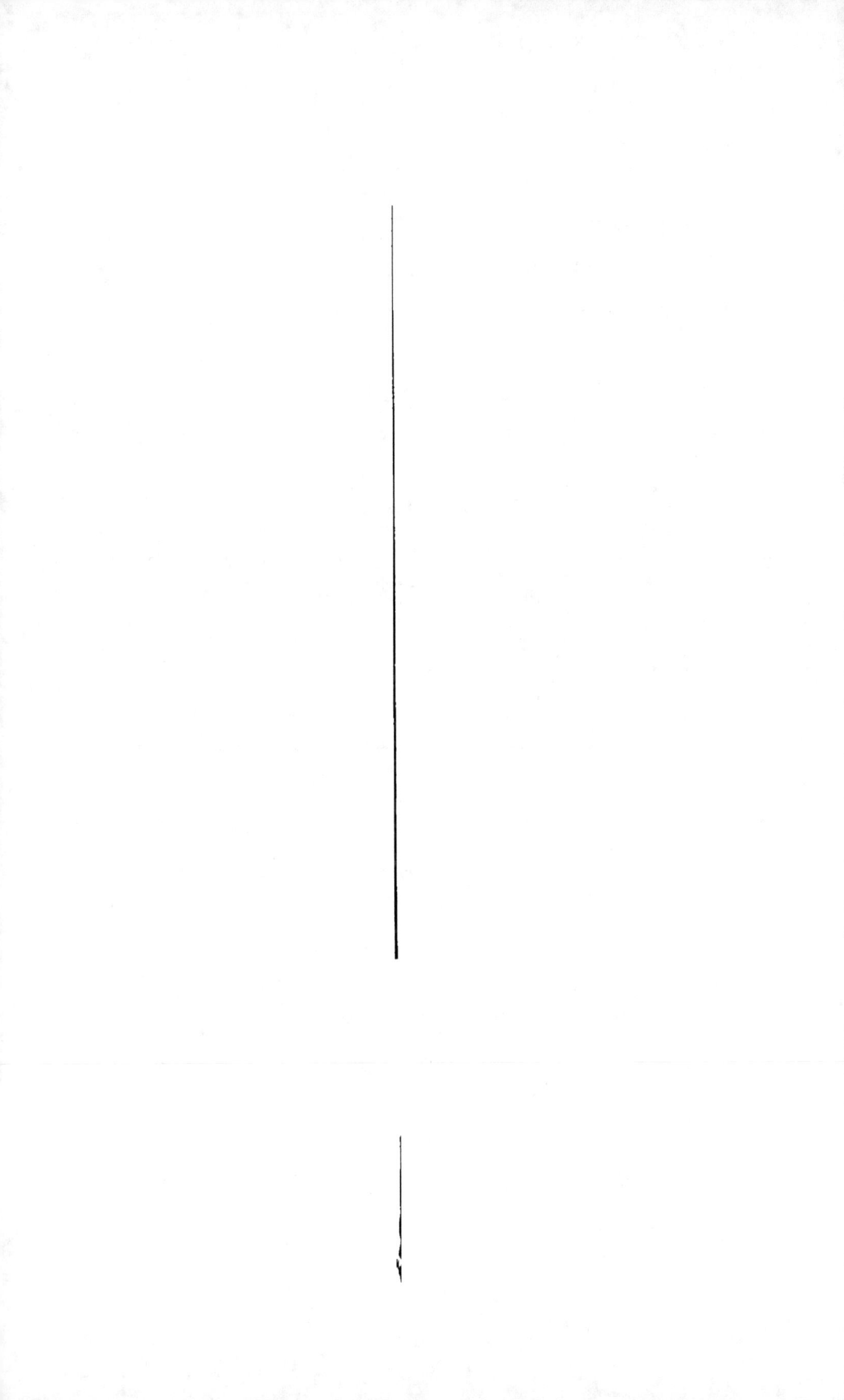

Wyld,sec.168 b,states that the rounded value (ø) was found in
13th and 15th century texts,although Mackenzie,sec176,says
that "in the City and Essex dialects,O.E. eo is monophthong-
ised directly to o,probably in L.O.E.".

(130) y
Heaney,"On Certain Features of the London Dialect in the 12th
Century",Eng.Stud.,vol.50,p.345,gives a summary of y:
In London and Middlesex of the 12th and 15th centuries,O.E.y
appears as i,e and u.There is evidence,already in the 12th cen
-tury,of unrounding to i,-a stage reached,probably,in the 10th
century.
On further details of the London dialect,he gives the following notes:
Both O.E. ēa and ē become slack (ɛ:).There is also a tendency
to o forms,but evidence is not sufficient to prove the existence of a tense (e:).
London and Middlesex were within the fracture area for O.E.ea
plus consonant,but the Angl.type appears in the 11th century,
and is the normal form in the 12th and 15th centuries.

(131) Pronouns.
Wyld,sec.512,"It/ seems evident that their comes into literary
English,through E. Mid. from the North".
See also note 70 above.

(132) Present Part.
Wyld,sec.557,"The earliest London documents have -inde;the
later charters have only -yng,-ing or -eng".

<u>Alliterative poetry.</u>

(133) To the D type (/ / \ X) and the E type (\ X / /),the
strong stresses of the O.E. compounds were necessary but,
with the influx of foreign synonyms at the end of the O.E. per
-iod,the need for alliterating words was not,and the compounds
disappeared.As Oakden says,"The old poetic compounds have disappeared,and with them the D and E types but otherwise the
metre remains the same"-Allit.Poetry.in M.E.,p.135

(134) The C type (X / / X) also frequently depended on what
Oakden calls "a compound double stress",and such 6 half-lines
disappeared at the same time as the D and E types,but the
type "when consisting of two separate stressed words" remained.
Oakden,Allit. Poetry,p.149.

(135) Sievers's metrical survey of Beowulf shows that the metrical tendency is predominantly trochaic,and of the trochaic
types,the A type is by far the most frequent.Vigfusson and
Powell (Corpus Poeticum Boreale) also note that "the last syllable of each Caedmonian half-line appear to have in preference
the quantity / X",p.435.

(I36) The influence of the loss of inflectional endings on
rhythms: Oakden,Allit. Poetry in M.E.,p.I76,points out that
"in earlier poems,such as Scottish Field,in which the final
'e' had been lost long before the time of writing,a change has
inevitably taken place;the line frequently ends in X / ".
Luick,commenting on this change of rhythm says,"This began
a new tradition in verse",-"Die Englische Stabreimzeile im
XIV,XV,und XVI Jahrhundert",Anglia,vol.IX,p.403.

(I37) The influence of the introduction of prepositions may
be seen from the following example:
   'cyningum' with its (/ X X) rhythm is changed to
   'to the kings' with (X X /).

(I38) The following lines show the shift from trochaic to
iambic rhythm.They are taken from O.E.,M.E. and L.M.E. texts.

     "Gōd mid Cēatum : Grendles dǣda", (Beowulf,1.24.)
      / X / X   / X / X

     "In a somer seson: whan soft was the sonne",(Piers the
      X X / X / X   X /   X X X/ X   Plowman,1.I)

"Bieten fires full fast; with leames full light" (Scottish
 X X / X X /   X   / X X   /   Fielde)

In the last poem,the real rhythm,whatever its source,is definitely of the B type.

(I39) The effect of lengthening.
The influence of lengthening appears in a comparatively limited field,but it affected greatly the O.E. phenomenon of re-
solution.Instead of two short vowels by resolution making up
one full stress,lengthening made them into one full stress
plus a following unstressed syllable.
That is,theoretically,the rhythm of the line:
       'to brimes faroþo' would become 'to brīmes faroþe'
        X ↲   ↲ X   X / X / X X
which is an a type with anacrusis leading toward the general
vague line of M.E. alliterative poetry.

(I40) Influence of shortening.
The influence of shortening on alliterative metres is seen in
connection with compounds,trisyllables and unstressed forms.T
The whole influence is toward an increase of thesis syllables
and a further tendency toward vague and generalised types.It
contributed to the loss of the C and D types dependent u on
compounds,and to the increase of unstressed thesis syllables
in types E and A. This last change contributes to the mer-
ging of the E type with A.

e.g. 'wisdome hoold' (Beo.1.1959)-D type , (/ /\ X)
beside
      'How Wysdom thorowe wantonnesse',Skelton,Magn. 194.
        X / X   X X / X X
where the thesis of the A type is increased through shortening.
    Moreover,the loss through shortening of large numbers of
syllables capable of bearing main or secondary stress tends
to give the line a quicker,lighter movement.Again,one of the
functions of the secondary stressed syllable was to link the
stressed and unstressed ones.The disappearance of this link
through shortening tends to produce a sharper distinction
between arsis and thesis,that is,a stronger feeling of accent.
See also,Luick,Die Stabreimzeile,Anglia,vol.IX,p.404;Schipper,
History of English Versification,pp.141 and 169.

(141) Oakden formulates the vague line of M.E. alliterative p
poetry in the following terms:
        (X X X) / (X) / (X X)

(142) In O.E. verse,the accent falls on a syllable which is
naturally long or which acquires length by means of the resolution of the following vowel into it.The fact that this
satisfying of the length of a syllable was customary seems to
imply a refutation of Dr.Guest's statement (History of Eng.
Rhythms,p.169) that "no temporal rhythms are to be found in
our literature".

(143) Early plays,see Pollard,Early English Miracle Plays,Int.

(144) Dating of M.E. documents,see Wyld,Short History,pp.99-104.

Bibliography

<u>exts.</u>

radley,Henry — The Making of English,1904.

lasson,H. — A History of the English Language,1919.

onybeare,.D. — Illustrations of Anglo-Saxon Poetry,1826.

merson,O.F. — 1. A Middle English Reader,1915
11. A History of the English Language,1894.

oster,T.F. — Judith:Studies in Metre, Language and Style,1892.

uest,E. — A History of English Rhythms,ed.Skeat,1882.

all,J. — Selections from Early Middle English,(2 vols.),1920.

uchon — Histoire de la Langue Anglais 2 vols.,1923,1930

esperson,O. — A Modern English Grammar, 5 vols.,1933.

ordan,R. — Handbuch der Mittelenglische Grammatik,ed.Matthes,1932.

aluza,M. — 1. Historische Grammatik der Englische Sprache,1907.
11. Short History of English Versification,(trans.Dunstan) 1911.

Lewellyn,C.C. — The Influence of Low Dutch on the English Vocabulary,Pub. Phil.Soc.,1936.

ounsbury — Studies in Chaucer,(3 vols.) 1892.

uick,K. — Historische Grammatik der Englische Sprache,1904.

Mackenzie,B.K.   Early London Dialect,1928.

Maclean,G.E.   Old and Middle English
                                        Reader,1893.

Menner,R.J.   ed. Purity,1920.

Moore,S.   Historical Outlines of Eng-
                                        lish Morphology and Phonology
                                        1925.

Morris,R.   Early English Alliterative
                                        Poems in the W.Mid. Dialect
                                        of the 14th Century,E.E.T.S.
                                        1864.

Morsbach,L.   Mittelenglische Grammatik,1896

New English Dictionary,1918.

Oakden,J.P.   Alliterative Poetry in Middle
                                        English,1930.

Pollard,A.   Early English Miracle Plays

Savage,L.   ed. St. Erkenwald,1926.

Schipper,J.   History of English Versifi-
                                        cation,1910.

Shorter Oxford Dictionary,1933.

Sweet,H.   History of English Sounds,1888

Skeat,W.W.   i.   ed. Piers the Plowman,10thed.
                                        Revised,1928 imp.

                                 ii.   Principles of English Etymo-
                                        logy,1891.

Ten Brink   The Language and Metre of
                                        Chaucer,1901 .

Tolkien,J.R. and Gordon,E.V.   ed. Gawayne and the Grene
                                        Knight,1925.

Vigfusson,G. and Powell,F.Y.   Corpus Poeticum Boreale(2 vols
                                        Excursion on Northern Metres
                                        vol.I,1883.

Wardale,E.   An Old English Grammar,1928

Wells,J.E.   A Manual of the Writings in
                                    M.E., 1916-1935.

Wright,J. and E.M.   i. An Old English Grammar,1925
                             ii. An Elementary Middle English
                                    Grammar,1927.

Wyld,H.C.   i. A Short History of English,
                                    1927.
                             ii. Historical Study of the Mother
                                    Tongue,1906.

Articles.

Andrew,S.O.   The preterite in the N.W. Dial-
                                    ects,Rev. of Eng. Studies,vol.5
                                    1929,pp.431-436.

Bush,S.H.   Old Northern French Loan-words
                                    in M.E.,Phil.Quarterly,vol.I,
                                    1922,pp.161-178.

Flom,G.E.   Anglo-Norman Sript and the Script
                                    Of Twelfth Century MSS. in North-
                                    eastern Norway,Studies in Honour
                                    of Frederick Klaeber,1929.

Heuser,W.   Zum Kent. Dialekt im Mitteleng-
                                    lischen,Anglia,vol.17,1895,
                                    pp.73-90.

Kaplan,T.H.   Gower's Vocabulary,M.L.R.,vol.31,
                                    1932,pp.395-403.

Langlans,Victor   Der Reimvokal o bei Chaucer,Anglia,
                                    vol.45,1921,pp.221-282,297-392.

Lindkvist,Harald   On the History of the English
                                    Pronoun 'sho',Anglia,vol.45,1921,
                                    pp. I-50.

Luick,K.   Die Englische Stabreimzeile in
                                    XIV,XV,und XVI Jahrhundert,Anglia,
                                    vol.IX,1889,pp.533-618.

ckenzie,B.X.   A Special Dialectal Development
                                 of O.E. ea in M.E.,Englische Stud.,
                                 vol.61,1926-27,pp.386-392.

lone,Kemp   When Did M.E. Begin?,Curme Volume
                                 of Linguistic Studies,Language
                                 Monographs,vol.7,pp.110-118.

nner,R.J.   Four Notes on the W.Midland Dia-
                                 lect,M.L.N.,vol.41,1926,pp.454-458.

ore,S.   Loss of Final n in the Inflect-
                                 ional Syllables of M.E.,Language,
                                 vol.IV,1928,pp.232-260.

gatscher,A.   Die Englische æ /e Grenze,Anglia,
                                 vol.XXIII,pp.206-220.

aney,P.H.   1.   On Certain Phonological Features
                                 of the Dialect of London in the
                                 Twelfth Century,Eng.Studien,vol.59,
                                 1925,pp.321-345.
                        11.   The Dialect of London in the Thir-
                                 teenth Century,Eng.St.,vol.61,1926
                                 pp.9-23.

rjeantson,M.S.   1.   The Development of O.E. eag/eah
                                 in M.E.,Journ.of Eng.and Gen.Phil.
                                 vol.26,1927,pp.198-226,350-451.
                        11.   The Dialect of(London in)the West
                                 Midlands,Rev. of Eng. St.,vol.3,
                                 1927,pp.54,184,319.

ylor,A.B.   On the History of O.E. ea/eo in
                                 Middle Kentish,M.L.R.,vol.19,
                                 1924,pp.1-10.

ld,H.C.   The Treatment of O.E. y in Dialects
                                 of Midland and South-eastern,Counties
                                 in M.E.,Eng.Stud.,vol.47,pp.1-59.

ohrisson,R.E.   The Early English Loan-words in
                                 Welsh and the Chronology of the
                                 English Sound Shift,Studies in
                                 English Philology in Honour of
                                 Frederick Klaeber,1929.

www.ingramcontent.com/pod-product-compliance
Lightning Source LLC
Chambersburg PA
CBHW051547030726
47592CB00001B/179